An Annotated Bibliography
of
John Dryden

An Annotated Bibliography of John Dryden:
Texts and Studies, 1949-1973

John A. Zamonski

Garland Publishing, Inc., New York & London

1975

Copyright © 1975

by Garland Publishing, Inc.

All Rights Reserved

PR
3423
.Z36
Z99

Library of Congress Cataloging in Publication Data

Zamonski, John A
   An annotated bibliography of John Dryden.

   Includes index.
   1. Dryden, John, 1631-1700--Bibliography.   I. Title.
Z8244.Z35   016.821'4   74-22231
ISBN 0-8240-1059-0

Printed in the United States of America

Contents

	Page
Preface	ix
Abbreviations	xi

I   CANON AND BIBLIOGRAPHY:

Authoritative Texts (#s 1-6)	1
School Texts:	
general (#s 7-12)	3
dramas (#s 13-18)	4
essays (#s 19-25)	4
poetry (#s 26-38)	5
translations (#s 39-41)	7
Reprints (#s 42-56)	7
Phonodiscs (#s 57-65)	9
Bibliographic Studies:	
catalogues (#s 66-8)	10
checklists and annotated bibliographies (#s 69-79)	11
concordances (#s 80-2)	13
textual studies:	
authorship (#s 83-6)	13
editing (#s 87-93)	14
textual criticism (#s 94-112)	15

II   BIOGRAPHY:

General Studies (#s 113-22)	17
Literary Relationships (#s 123-34)	19
Religion (#s 135-40)	21

CONTENTS

III	COMPREHENSIVE OR MISCELLANEOUS STUDIES: (#s 141-82)	22
IV	DRAMA:	

Comprehensive and Miscellaneous Subjects (#s 183-218)	27
On the Prologues and Epilogues (#s 219-23)	31
On the Comedies (#s 224-44)	32
On Heroic Drama (#s 245-82)	35
On the Operas (#s 283-5)	41
On the Tragedies (#s 286-98)	41
On Specific Dramas, by title (#s 299-444)	43

V   PROSE:

General Studies (#s 445-7)	63
On the Dedications (#s 448-54)	63
A Defence of the Papers Written by the Late King of Blessed Memory and Duchess of York (#455)	64
On the Letters (#s 456-61)	65
On the Literary Criticism and Theory: comprehensive and miscellaneous studies (#s 462-504)	66
on specific essays, by title (#s 505-65)	72
On Prose Style (#s 566-78)	81

VI   POETRY:

Comprehensive and Miscellaneous Studies (#s 579-631)	83
On the Elegies:	
comprehensive study (#632)	90
on specific elegies, by title (#s 633-54)	90
Epistles in Verse	
comprehensive studies (#s 655-6)	93

CONTENTS

on specific epistles, by title (#s 657-70)	94
The Miscellanies (#671)	96
The Odes:	
Mrs. Anastasia Stafford (# 672)	96
St. Cecilia's Day odes:	
dual studies (#s 673-7)	97
Alexander's Feast (#s 678-82)	97
Song for St. Cecilia's Day, 1687 (#683-7)	98
On the Public Panegyrics:	
general studies (#s 688-96)	99
on specific panegyrics:	
Annus Mirabilis (#s 697-708)	101
Astraea Redux (#s 709-13)	102
Heroique Stanzas (#741)	103
On the Religious Poems:	
The Hind and the Panther (#s 715-43)	103
Religio Laici (#s 744-69)	108
On Satirical Poetry:	
comprehensive and miscellaneous studies (#s 770-83)	111
On specific satires:	
Absalom and Achitophel (#s 784-847)	113
Mac Flecknoe (#s 848-83)	121
The Medall (#s 884-92)	125
VII TRANSLATIONS:	
General Studies (#s 893-8)	127
The *Fables* (#s 899-901)	128
On Translations of Specific Authors (#s 902-79)	128
Index of Authors, Editors, and Reviewers	140

Preface

It has been nearly 25 years since the appearance of Samuel Holt Monk's *John Dryden: a List of Critical Studies Published from 1895 to 1948* (Minneapolis, 1950). Since that time the volume of Dryden scholarship has grown considerably, and from it emerge two important results: authoritative texts and the revaluation of Dryden's artistry. L. A. Beaurline and Fredson Bowers have applied modern bibliographic principles to provide critical editions of eight of the plays. James Kinsley's *The Poems of John Dryden*, 4 vols. (Oxford, 1958) is a milestone; more so is *The Works of John Dryden* (Berkeley, 1956-) begun by Edward Niles Hooker. Eight volumes are in print and a ninth (Vol. XVIII: *Prose, The History of the League*) is scheduled for publication later this year. The volumes are old-spelling, critical editions by computer assisted teams of scholars. Regarding the criticism close readings of the literature and more comprehensive studies have strongly illustrated the integrity of Dryden's protean career.

This bibliography chronicles a generation of work and is intended for all those from scholar to casual student interested in Dryden. It gathers into one volume an annotated, categorized, and cross-referenced list of texts and studies from 1949 to 1973. Its descriptive character should serve a broad range of needs. True, the presentation of the material conveys judgments but the quotes allow the articles and dissertations to speak for themselves and to the point. In the case of the books, I have cited what I hope will be reviews sufficient to provide a balance of opinion.

I have examined the annual bibliographies published by the Modern Humanities Research Association, the Modern

PREFACE

Language Association, and *Philological Quarterly*, and lists in publications of more limited scopes. I have used Lawrence F. McNamee's *Dissertations in English and American Literature* (New York, 1968-), now in its second supplement, and have taken quoted material from *Dissertation Abstracts International*, Ann Arbor. Also of use were the bibliographies of Louis C. Gatto (see #72 within) and Carl J. Stratman, S.J. (#79). I have examined the majority of the books and articles cited; the collection of the data began in 1969 and my knowledge of many of the items dates back to 1959.

Acknowledgements:

I wish to express my gratitude to many for their encouragement and assistance, particularly my wife, Kathleen. My thanks to the following here at Wright State University: A. K. M. Aminul Islam, Associate Professor of Sociology, Anthropology, and Social Work, for help with translations; Grover Brooks, Lynn K. Chmelir, and Richard S. Tyce, Instructors of Library Administration and Reference Librarians, for their prompt attention to numerous inquiries. I am grateful to the College of Liberal Arts and Dean Eugene B. Cantelupe for a research grant. And I am indebted to the following faculty of the English Department, Ohio University, Athens: Frank B. Fieler directed my earliest attempts at bibliography; John A. Jones encouraged my interest in Dryden; and, Calvin G. Thayer strongly influenced my attitudes toward seventeenth-century literature.

Dayton, Ohio
September 1, 1974

John A. Zamonski

ABBREVIATIONS

ANQ	American Notes and Queries
Archiv	Archiv für das Studium der Neueren Sprachen und Litteraturen
AnR	Antioch Review
Ar	Ariel; a Review of International English Literature
AUMLA	Journal of the Australasian Universities Language and Literature Association
BA	Books Abroad
BC	Book Collector
BNYPL	Bulletin of the New York Public Library
BR	Bucknell Review
BSUF	Ball State University Forum
CamJ	Cambridge Journal
CamQ	Cambridge Quarterly
CamR	Cambridge Review
CCLC	Cuadernos del Congresso por la Libertad de la Cultura
CD	Comparative Drama
CE	College English
CEA	CEA Critic
CJ	Classical Journal
CLAJ	College Language Association Journal
CL	Comparative Literature
CLS	Comparative Literature Studies
CP	Concerning Poetry
CQR	Church Quarterly Review
CR	Chaucer Review
CritQ	Critical Quarterly
Crit	Critical Survey
CSE	Cairo Studies in English
DalR	Dalhousie Review
DC	Drama Critique
DS	Drama Survey
DUJ	Durham University Journal
EA	Études Anglaises
ECS	Eighteenth-Century Studies
EE	Enlightenment Essays
EIC	Essays in Criticism
EigoS	Eigo Seinen
ELH	Journal of English Literary History
ELN	English Language Notes
ER	English Record
ES	English Studies
ESA	English Studies in Africa
ETJ	Educational Theatre Journal
EUQ	Emory University Quarterly
Exp	Explicator

HAB	Humanities Association Bulletin
HLQ	Huntington Library Quarterly
HSL	Hartford Studies in Literature
HTR	Harvard Theological Review
IEY	Iowa English Yearbook
JEGP	Journal of English and Germanic Philology
JWCI	Journal of the Warburg and Cortauld Institutes
LB	Leuv Bijdr
LS	Language and Style
MA	Modern Age
ML	Modern Languages
MLN	Modern Language Notes
MLQ	Modern Language Quarterly
MLR	Modern Language Review
MP	Modern Philology
MQ	Milton Quarterly
MQR	Michigan Quarterly Review
MS	Milton Studies
N&Q	Notes and Queries
NRMS	Nottingham Renaissance and Modern Studies
NSt	New Statesman
NYTBR	New York Times Book Review
OR	Oxford Review
PBSA	Papers of the Bibliographic Society of America
PLL	Papers on Language and Literature
PLPLSLHS	Proceedings of the Leeds Philosophical and Literary Society, Literary and Historical Section
PMLA	Publications of the Modern Language Association
QQ	Queen's Quarterly
RECTR	Restoration and 18th Century Theatre Research
RES	Review of English Studies
RLC	Revue de Littérature Comparée
RLMC	Rivista di Letterature Moderne e Comparate
RLV	Revue des Langues Vivantes
SAB	South-Atlantic Bulletin
SB	Studies in Bibliography
SCB	South-Central Bulletin
SCN	Seventeenth-Century News
SEL	Studies in English Literature
Sew Rev	Sewanee Review
SHR	Scottish Historical Review
SJ	Shakespeare-Jahrbuch
SLing	Studies in English Literature
SN	Shakespeare Newsletter
SNL	Satire Newsletter
SP	Studies in Philology
SQ	Shakespeare Quarterly

SSJ	Southern Speech Journal
TA	Theatre Annual
TLS	Times Literary Supplement
TN	Theatre Notebook
TS	Theatre Survey
TSE	Tulane Studies in English
TSLL	Texas Studies in Literature and Language
UDR	University of Dayton Review
UTQ	University of Toronto Quarterly
UTSE	[University of] Texas Studies in English
WC	Wordsworth Circle
WW	Wirkendes Wort
YR	Yale Review
YES	Yearbook of English Studies

AN ANNOTATED BIBLIOGRAPHY OF JOHN DRYDEN: TEXTS AND STUDIES, 1949-1973

I CANON AND BIBLIOGRAPHY:

Authoritative Texts

1 Beaurline, L. A., and Fredson Bowers, eds. John Dryden: Four Comedies. (Curtain Playwrights.) Chicago and London: The University of Chicago Press; Toronto: The University of Toronto Press, 1967. ix + 367pp.

   Critical, old-spelling texts of Secret Love, Sir Martin Mar-all, An Evening's Love, and Marriage a-la-Mode. Introduction, 1-22; bibliography, 365-7. Reviewed in SCN, XXVII, 28; by Philip Roberts in N&Q, XVI, 933-4; by Phillip Harth in MP, LXVII, 379-82; and, by P. K. Elkin in AUMLA, XXXVI, 210-16.

2 _____. John Dryden: Four Tragedies. (Curtain Playwrights.) Chicago and London: The University of Chicago Press; Toronto: The University of Toronto Press, 1967. ix + 412pp.

   Critical, old-spelling texts of The Indian Emperour, Aureng-Zebe, All for Love, and Don Sebastian. Introduction, 1-25; bibliography, 409-12. Reviewed in SCN, XXVII, 28; and by Phillip Harth in MP, LXVII, 379-82.

3 Kinsley, James, ed. The Poems of John Dryden. 4 vols. (Oxford English Texts.) Oxford: The Clarendon Press, 1958. xi + 2104pp.

   Critical edition of the complete poems. Reviewed by George Watson in JEGP, LVIII, 530-3; by V. de S. Pinto in MLR, LIV, 592-4; by Pierre Legouis in EA, XII, 353-4; by D. M. Vieth in MP, LVI, 279-82; by John Wilders in CamR, LXXX, 147, 149, 151; by A. Alvarez in NSt, LVII, 18-19; in TLS, Jan. 16, 1959, 32; and, by John Butt in RES, XI, 213-15. (See also #s 590 and 616 below.)

4 Noyes, George R., ed. The Poetical Works of Dryden. Revised and enlarged edition. (The Cambridge Edition of the Poets.) Boston: Houghton Mifflin Company, 1950. lxxii + 1095pp.

   Critical edition of the poems. Reviewed in TLS, Feb. 16, 1951, 93-5.

5 Stroup, Thomas B., and Arthur L. Cooke, eds. The Works of Nathaniel Lee. 2 vols. New Brunswick, N. J., 1954-5; Metuchen, N. J.: Scarecrow Reprint Corporation, 1968.

A critical, old-spelling edition, including Oedipus, vol.
I, 367-449, and The Duke of Guise, vol. II, 387-476. Reviewed in SCN, XIII, 41; in N&Q, II, 320-1; and, by Fredson Bowers in PQ, XXXV, 310-14.

6   The Works of John Dryden. H. T. Swedenberg, Jr., general editor; Earl Miner, associate general editor; Vinton A. Dearing, textual editor; and, George R. Guffey, associate textual editor. Berkeley and Los Angeles: University of California Press, 1956-

The definitive edition in progress, the California Dryden is a critical, old-spelling edition projected to 20 volumes. (See #s 87-8 and 90-1 below.)

Vol. I: Poems, 1649-1680. Edward Niles Hooker, H. T. Swedenberg, Jr., and Vinton A. Dearing, eds.; Frederick M. Carey, Godfrey Davies, Hugh G. Dick, Samuel Holt Monk, and John Harrington Smith, assoc. eds. 1956. xviii + 414pp. Reviewed by James M. Osborn in PQ, XXXVI, 358-9;by H. Sikes in SCN, XIV, 2; by Calvin G. Thayer in BA, XXXI, 193; by D. M. Knight in CE, XVIII, 290; by Vivian de Sola Pinto in MLR, LII, 590-2; by James Kinsley in RES, VIII, 445-8; by Charles E. Ward in MP, LV, 129-32; by Pierre Legouis in EA, XI, 54-6; and, by John Wilders in CamR, LXXX, 147, 149, 151.

Vol. II: Poems, 1681-1684. H. T. Swedenberg, Jr., and Vinton A. Dearing, eds. 1972. xiv + 488pp. Reviewed in SCN, XXXI, 3; and by Phillip Harth in PQ, LII, 492-3.

Vol. III: Poems, 1685-1692. Earl Miner and Vinton A. Dearing, eds.; Norman Austin, Samuel Holt Monk, and Thomas G. Rosenmeyer, assoc. eds. 1969. xvi + 581pp. Reviewed in TLS, Sept. 4, 1970, 977; by George McFadden in PQ, XLIX, 340-1. (See also #728 below.)

Vol. VIII: Plays, The Wild Gallant, The Rival Ladies, The Indian Queen. John Harrington Smith, Dougald MacMillan, and Vinton A. Dearing, eds.; Samuel Holt Monk and Earl Miner, assoc. eds. 1962. xii + 376pp. Reviewed in TLS, Mar. 22, 1963, 196; by Vivian de Sola Pinto in MLR, LVIII, 241-3; in PQ, XLII, 344-5; by E. A. Langhans in TN, XVII, 94-7; by Cecil Price in Neuphilologische Mitteilungen, LXV, 108-9; and, by Clarence Tracy in QQ, LXX, 286-7.

Vol. IX: Plays, The Indian Emperour, Secret Love, Sir Martin Mar-all. John Loftis and Vinton A. Dearing, eds. viii + 451pp. Reviewed by John Freehafer in TN, XXIII, 34-5; by Philip Roberts in N&Q, XVI, 115-17; by Pierre Legouis in EA, XXII, 193-4; and, by Arthur C. Kirsch in

PQ, XLVI, 340-1

Vol. X: *Plays, The Tempest, Tyrannick Love, An Evening's Love*. Maximillian E. Novak and George R. Guffey, eds. 1970. x + 557pp. Reviewed in TLS, July 30, 1971, 916; by William Myers in RES, XXIII, 357-60; and, by Arthur C. Kirsch in PQ, L, 426-7.

Vol. XVII: *Prose, 1668-1691*. Samuel Holt Monk, A. E. Wallace Maurer, and Vinton A. Dearing, eds.; R. V. LeClercq and Maximillian E. Novak, assoc. eds. 1971. xii + 528pp. Reviewed by John R. Clark in SCN, XXXI, 3.

School Texts:

general

7 Frost, William, ed. *John Dryden: Selected Works*. 2d ed. (Rinehart Editions, 60.) San Francisco: Rinehart Press, 1971. xxxix + 517pp.

   Chronology, xxiii-xxxviii. First edition, 1953, reviewed by N. Joost in Poetry, LXXXVI, 120-1.

8 Grant, Douglas, ed. *Poems and Prose of John Dryden: a Selection*. (The Penguin Poets.) Baltimore and Harmondsworth: Penguin Books, Inc., 1955. 357pp.

   Reviewed in SCN, XIV, 8; in TLS, Oct. 28, 1955, 634; by Pierre Legouis in EA, IX, 350; and, by A. L. McLeod in BA, XXX, 333.

9 _____. *Dryden: Poetry, Prose, and Plays*. Cambridge, Mass.: Harvard University Press; London: Hart-Davis, Ltd.; Toronto: Clarke-Irwin, 1952. 896pp.

   Reviewed in Listener, XLVII, 1053; in TLS, Feb. 1, 1952, 94; and, by Pierre Legouis in EA, V, 359-60.

10 Miner, Earl, ed. *Selected Poetry and Prose of John Dryden*. (Modern Library College Editions.) New York: Random House, Inc., 1969. 554pp.

11 Thomas, Donald, ed. *A Selection from John Dryden*. (Longman English Series.) London: Longman, 1972. vii + 228pp. (Bibliography, 228.)

12 Zesmer, David, ed. *Dryden: Poems, Plays, and Essays*. (Bantam Classics.) New York: Bantam Books, 1967. 529pp. (Bibliography, 525-9.)

dramas
(See #s 354 and 415 below)

13   Enck, John J., ed. *All for Love; or, The World Well Lost*.
     (Crofts Classics.) New York: Appleton-Century-Crofts,
     1966. xxxix + 86pp. (Bibliography, 86.)

14   Griffith, Benjamin W., Jr., ed. *All for Love; or, The
     World Well Lost*. (Theatre Classics for the Modern
     Reader.) Great Neck, N.Y.: Barron's Educational
     Series, 1961. 156pp.

     Bibliography, 155-6. Illustrated by Tom Keogh.

15   Kaufmann, R. J., ed. *All for Love*. San Francisco:
     Chandler Publishing Co., 1962. 78pp.

     Introduction reprinted as "On the Poetics of Terminal
     Tragedy: Dryden's *All for Love*," in #145 below, 86-94.

16   Link, Frederick M., ed. *Aureng-Zebe*. (Regents Restora-
     tion Drama Series.) Lincoln: University of Nebraska
     Press, 1971. xxiii + 131pp. (Has a Dryden Chronology.)

17   Sale, Arthur, ed. *All for Love*. 2d ed. London: Univer-
     sity Tutorial Press, 1961. xxiii + 223pp. (Bibliogra-
     phical notes, 105-223.)

18   Vieth, David M., ed. *All for Love*. (Regents Restoration
     Drama Series.) Lincoln: University of Nebraska Press,
     1972. xxxiv + 146pp.

     Reviewed by Derek Cohen in SCN, XXXI, #1.

essays

19   Aden, John M., comp. and ed. *The Critical Opinions of
     John Dryden*: a Dictionary. Nashville: Vanderbilt
     University Press, 1963. xxviii + 292pp.

     Reviewed by James L. Clifford in Sat Rev, Aug 10, 1963,
     32, 55; by C. J. Rawson in N&Q, X, 439-40; by James
     Kinsley in MLR, LIX, 111; by Donald F. Bond in MP, LXII,
     72-5; and, in TLS, Jan. 23, 1964, 69.

20   Boulton, James T., ed. *Of Dramatic Poesie: an Essay*.
     With Sir Robert Howard's *Preface to The Great Favourite*
     and Dryden's. *Defence of an Essay*. London: Oxford Uni-
     versity Press, 1964. 190pp.

     A chronological outline, 21-4; bibliography, 25.

21 Kinsley, James, and George Parfitt, eds. John Dryden:
    Selected Criticism. (Oxford Paperback English Texts.)
    Oxford: The Clarendon Press; New York: Oxford University Press, 1970. xix + 315pp.

    Bibliography, xix. Reviewed in ES, LIV, 393-5; and by
    Roger Lonsdale in N&Q, XX, 197-8.

22 Kirsch, Arthur C., ed. Literary Criticism of John Dryden.
    (Regents Critics Series.) Lincoln: University of Nebraska Press, 1966. xvii + 174pp.

    Bibliography, 171. Reviewed by Leslie Howard Martin in
    SCN, XXV, 70-1.

23 Mahoney, John L., ed. An Essay of Dramatic Poesy, A Defence of an Essay of Dramatic Poesy, Preface to the
    Fables. (Library of Liberal Arts.) Indianapolis: The
    Bobbs-Merrill Company, Inc., 1965. xxi + 119pp. (Bibliography, xix-xx.)

24 Mirizzi, Piero, ed. John Dryden: Saggi Critici. (Biblioteca Italiana di Testi Inglesi, 14.) Bari: Adriatica Editrice, 1968. 359pp.

    Introduction and notes, 1-90; bibliography, 103-9. The
    selections are in English.

25 Watson, George, ed. John Dryden: Of Dramatic Poesy and
    Other Critical Essays. 2 vols. (Everyman's Library,
    568-9.) London: J. M. Dent & Sons, Ltd.; New York: E.
    P. Dutton and Company, 1962. xxvi + 279; vi + 322pp.

    Bibliography, xix-xx. Reviewed by Donald F. Bond in MP,
    LXII, 72-3.

                              poetry

26 Arthos, John, ed. John Dryden: Selected Poetry. (The
    Signet Classic Poetry Series.) New York: New American
    Library, 1970. xxx + 31-352pp. (Bibliography, xxix-xxx.)

27 Auden, W. H., ed. A Choice of Dryden Verse. London:
    Faber and Faber Limited, 1973. 115pp.

28 Brower, Reuben A., ed. Dryden. (The Laurel Poetry Series.) New York: Dell Publishing Co., Inc., 1962.
    160pp. (Bibliography, 19-20.)

29 Elloway, D. R., ed. Dryden's Satire. (English Classics,
    New Series.) London: The Macmillan Company, Ltd.;

New York: St. Martin's Press, 1966. lvi + 182pp.

Bibliography, 182. Contains Mac Flecknoe, Absalom and Achitophel, and The Medal.

30   Frye, B. J., ed. Mac Flecknoe. (The Merrill Literary Casebook Series.) Columbus: Charles E. Merrill, 1970. v + 154pp.

Bibliography, 145-6. With critical essays (see #s 849, 868, and 870 below).

31   Gardner, Stanley, ed. John Dryden: Selected Poems. Oxford: Basil Blackwell, 1965. iv + 123pp.

32   Gardner, William Bradford, ed. The Prologues and Epilogues of John Dryden: A Critical Edition. New York: Columbia University Press; London: Oxford University Press, 1951. xxii + 361pp.

In this old-spelling edition of the complete prologues and epilogues, Gardner's copy-texts are the last printings known to have been revised by Dryden. Reviewed by Vivian de Sola Pinto in MLR, XLVII, 224; by James Kinsley in RES, III, 397-9; and, by Hoyt Trowbridge in MLN, LXVIII, 428-9.

33   Grigson, Geoffrey, ed. Selected Poems of John Dryden. (Crown Classics Series.) London: Grey Walls Press, 1950. 62pp. (Reviewed in TLS, Sept., 22, 1950, 603.)

34   Jones, Gwyn, ed. Songs and Poems of John Dryden. London: The Golden Cockerel Press, 1957. 64pp.

A limited edition of 500 numbered copies illustrated by Lavinia Blythe (copies 1-100 with an extra set of 16 illustrations handbound by Sangorski and Sutcliffe). Reviewed in TLS, Aug. 23, 1957, 509.

35   Kinsley, James, ed. The Poems and Fables of John Dryden. (Oxford Standard Authors.) London: Oxford University Press, 1962. xii + 864pp.

The text is that of #3 above, but without the explanatory notes. Reviewed in TLS, Mar. 9, 1962, 154; and by E. E. Duncan-Jones in MLR, LIX, 110-11.

36   Kinsley, James and Helen, eds. Absalom and Achitophel. London and New York: Oxford University Press, 1961. 65pp.

37   Sharrock, Roger, ed. Selected Poems of John Dryden. 2d ed. (Poetry Bookshelf.) London: Heinemann Educational

Books, Ltd., 1968. vi + 156pp.

Bibliography, 23. Reviewed in #606 below.

38 Strachey, J. St. Loe, ed. John Dryden: Poems. (The Nelson Classics.) London and New York: Thomas Nelson & Sons, Ltd., 1961 xvi + 347pp.

translations

39 Fitzgerald, R., ed. The Aeneid. Translated by Dryden. New York: The Macmillan Company, 1965. 416pp. (Bibliography, 416.)

40 Kinsley, James, ed. The Works of Virgil. Translated by John Dryden. London: Oxford University Press, 1961 xvi + 487pp.

A modern-spelling text of the Pastorals, Georgics, and Aeneid, not annotated fully.

41 Robinson, Charles Alexander, Jr., ed. Plutarch, Eight Great Lives: The Dryden Translation, Revised by Arthur Hugh Clough. (Rinehart Editions.) New York: Holt, Rinehart and Winston, Inc., 1960. xv + 364pp.

Reprints

42 Dryden, John. Absalom and Achitophel, 1681; The Second Part of Absalom and Achitophel, 1682. (A Scolar Press Facsimile.) Menston: The Scolar Press, 1970. 77pp.

Reviewed by John R. Clark in SCN, XXVIII, 51-2.

43 _____. All for Love, 1678. (A Scolar Press Facsimile.) Menston: The Scolar Press, 1969. 103pp.

The first edition, London, H. Herringman.

44 _____. "Tout pour l'amour, et le monde bien perdu, ou La mort d'Antoine et de Cleopatre, tragedie." Traduite de l'Anglois de Dryden. Oeuvres de A. -F. Prevost. T. 33, ptie. 2. Geneve: Slatkine Reprints, 1969. 231-407pp.

45 _____. Amphitryon; or, the Two Socias. A comedy, as it is acted at the Theatre Royal. To which is added the musick of the songs compos'd by Henry Purcel. London: Printed for J. Tonson, 1691; Rochester: University of Rochester Press, 1954.

Collation of the original: 2 vols. in 1, on 2 microcards.

46 _____. Antony and Cleopatra, 1813: With Alterations and with Additions from Dryden. (Attributed to J. P. Kemble and George Colman.) London: Cornmarket Press, Ltd., 1970. 80pp. (Facsimile.)

47 _____. Fables, 1700. Introduction by James Kinsley. (A Scolar Press Facsimile.) Menston: The Scolar Press, 1973.

48 _____. The Georgics: Translated into English Verse by John Dryden. Introduction by George F. Whicher. Verona: The Limited Editions Club, 1952; New York: The Heritage Press, 1953. xv + 154pp.

Illustrated by Bruno Bramanti. The limited edition was 1,500 copies.

49 _____. His Majesties Declaration Defended, 1681. Introduction by Godfrey Davies. (Augustan Reprint Society, 23.) Los Angeles: William Andrews Clark Memorial Library, University of California, 1950; New York: Kraus Reprint Corp., 1967. v + 20pp. (Facsimile.)

50 _____. The Indian Emperour, 1667. (A Scolar Press Facsimile.) Menston: The Scolar Press, 1971. 80pp.

The first edition, London, H. Herringman.

51 _____. Metamorphoses in Fifteen Books. Translated into English Verse under the Direction of Sir Samuel Garth by John Dryden, Alexander Pope, Joseph Addison, William Congreve, and Other Eminent Hands. New York: The Limited Editions Club, 1958; The Heritage Press, 1961. lvi + 519pp.

Introduction by Gilbert Highet; illustrated by Hans Erni. The limited edition was 1,500 copies.

52 _____. Of Dramatic Poesie, 1668. (A Scolar Press Facsimile.) Menston: The Scolar Press, 1969. 72pp.

53 _____. Sylvae, 1685. Introduction by James Kinsley. (A Scolar Press Facsimile.) Menston: The Scolar Press, 1973.

54 _____, and Sir William Davenant. The Tempest; or, The Enchanted Island, 1670. London: Cornmarket Press, Ltd., 1969. 83pp. (Facsimile.)

55 _____. "The Tempest," in After The Tempest, edited

by George R. Guffey. (Augustan Reprint Society.) Los Angeles: William Andrews Clark Memorial Library, University of California, 1969.

The 1670 edition, together with The Tempest; or, The Enchanted Island, 1674; The Mock-Tempest; or, The Enchanted Castle, 1675; and, The Tempest. An Opera, 1756.

56 Dryden, John. Troilus and Cressida; or, Truth Found too Late, 1679. (A Scolar Press Facsimile.) Menston: The Scolar Press, 1969. 70pp.

Phonodiscs

57 _____. Alexander's Feast. Music by George Frederic Handel. (Vanguard, S-282-3.) New York: Vanguard Recording Society, 1964. 4 sides.

Performed by Honor Sheppard, Max Writhley, Maurice Bevan, and, The Oriana Concert Choir & Orchestra, Alfred Deller, conductor. Notes by S. W. Bennell.

58 _____. All for Love; or, The World Well Lost. (A Classic Theatre Guild Production, LLP-4007.) New Rochelle, N. Y.: Library Editions, Request Records, Inc., n.d. 2 sides.

Directed by Elayne Carroll and Robert M. Culp.

59 _____, and Sir Robert Howard. The Indian Queen. Music by Henry Purcell. Edited by Anthony Bernard. (Music Guild, MS-124.) Los Angeles: Music Guild Records, Westminster Record Co., n.d. 2 sides.

Performed by Patricia Clark, Cynthia Glover, Sylvia Rowlands, Bernard Baboulene, Duncan Roberston, John Whitworth, Frederick Westcott, James Atkins, The London Chamber Singers, Lionel Bentley, leader, and The London Chamber Orchestra, Anthony Bernard, conductor.

60 _____. The Indian Queen. Music by Henry Purcell. (L'Oiseau-Lyre, SOL-294.) London: Éditions de L'Oiseau-Lyre, The Decca Records Company Limited, 1966. 2 sides.

Performed by Wilfred Brown, April Cantelo, Robert Tear, Christopher Keyte, Ian Partridge, The St. Anthony Singers, John McCarthy, chorus master, The English Chamber Orchestra, Emanuel Hurwitz, leader, Charles Mackerras, conductor. Notes by Charles Cudworth.

61   Dryden, John. John Dryden. (The English Poets from Chaucer to Yeats, ZPL-1027.) London: Argo Record Company, Limited, 1971. 2 sides.

Read by William Devlin, Freda Dowie, David King, and Richard Pasco. Directed by George Rylands and recorded in association with the British Council and Oxford University Press.

62   _____. King Arthur; or, The British Worthy. A Dramatic Opera. Music by Henry Purcell. (L'Oiseau-Lyre, SOL-60008-9.) London: Éditions de L'Oiseau-Lyre, The Decca Records Company Limited, 1960. 4 sides.

Performed by Elsie Morison, Heather Harper, Mary Thomas, John Whitworth, David Galliver, Wilfred Brown, John Cameron, Hervey Alan, Trevor Anthony, The St. Anthony Singers, and, The Orchestra of the Philomusica of London, Anthony Lewis, conductor. With Dryden's dedication; libretto and program notes by Nigel Fortune.

63   _____. Ode for St. Cecilia's Day. Music by George Frideric Handel. (Argo, ZRG-563.) London: Argo Records Company, Limited, n.d. 2 sides.

A Song for St. Cecilia's Day, 1687. Performed by April Cantelo and Ian Partridge with The Choir of King's College, Cambridge. Notes by Charles Cudworth.

64   _____. The Poetry of John Dryden. (Caedmon, TC-1125; CDL-51125.) New York: Caedmon Records Inc., n.d. 2 sides or 1 cassette. (Read by Paul Scofield.)

65   _____. A Treasury of John Dryden. (Spoken Arts, SA-866.) New Rochelle, N. Y.: Spoken Arts, 1964. 2 sides. (Read by Robert Speaight.)

Bibliographic Studies

catalogues

66   Crum, Margaret, comp. and ed. First Line Index of English Poetry, 1500-1800, in Manuscripts of the Bodleian Library, Oxford. 2 vols. Oxford: The Clarendon Press, 1969. 1-630; 631-1257pp.

Indexed by (1) Authors, (2) Shelf Marks, (3) Names Mentioned, (4) Authors of Works Translated, Paraphrased, or Imitated, and (5) Reference to Composers of Settings and Tunes Named or Quoted. Contains 77 Dryden entries.

67 Nicoll, Allardyce. <u>A History of English Drama</u>, 1660-1900.
    Vol. VI: A Short-Title Alphabetical Catalogue of Plays
    Produced or Printed in England from 1660 to 1900. Cambridge: Cambridge University Press, 1959. xii + 565pp.

    The guide to the first 5 vols. (fourth edition, revised, 1952) indicates authors and titles, "together with the years of original production, publication or submission to the licensing authority," and can be used as an independent reference.

68 Van Lennep, William, ed. <u>The London Stage</u>, 1660-1800.
    Part I: 1660-1700. Critical introduction by Emmett L. Avery and Arthur H. Scouten. Carbondale: Southern Illinois University Press, 1965. clxxv + 532 + clxxix.

    "A Calendar of Plays, Entertainments and Afterpieces, together with Casts, Box Receipts and Contemporary Comment. Compiled from the Playbills, Newspapers and Theatrical Diaries of the Period."

                    checklists
                       and
              annotated bibliographies

69 Bond, Donald F., comp. <u>The Age of Dryden</u>. (Goldentree Bibliographies in Language and Literature.) New York: Appleton-Century-Crofts, 1970. Pp. 7-22.

    A checklist of 289 items, texts and studies, mainly recent.

70 Browne, Ray B. "Dryden and Milton in Nineteenth-century Popular Songbooks," Bulletin of Bibliography, XXII (1958), 143-4.

    A checklist of 12 Dryden and 21 Milton titles.

71 Cameron, William James. <u>John Dryden in New Zealand; an Account of Early Editions of the Writings of John Dryden (1631-1700) Found in Various Libraries throughout New Zealand</u>. (Library School Bulletin, 1.) Wellington: Wellington Library School, National Library Service, 1960. 31pp.

    "Together with a list of English books in the University of Auckland printed before 1700 and a list of early Maori publications in the private collection of Mr. G. C. Petersen." A checklist with supplements to Hugh MacDonald's <u>John Dryden: A Bibliography of Early Editions and of Drydeniana</u> (Oxford, 1939), and James M. Osborn's

"Macdonald's Bibliography of Dryden: An Annotated Check-List of Selected American Libraries," in MP, XXXIX, 69-98, 197-212, and 313-19.

72 Gatto, Louis C. "An Annotated Bibliography of Critical Thought Concerning Dryden's Essay of Dramatic Poesy," RECTR, V (May, 1966), 18-29. (80 entries.)

73 Jackson, Allan S. "Bibliography of 17th and 18th Century Play Editions in the Rare Book Room of the Ohio State University Library," RECTR, VIII (May, 1969), 30-58.

See #s 80-103: several later editions; vols. I and II of the 1701 folio; no entries for The Indian Queen, The Indian Emperour, Tyrannick Love, The Conquest of Granada, The State of Innocence, The Mistaken Husband, The Kind Keeper, Albion and Albanius, Amphitryon, and The Secular Masque.

74 Keast, W. R. "Dryden Studies: 1895-1948," MP, XLVIII (1951), 205-10.

A review of Samuel Holt Monk's checklist (see #77 below) with 119 additions to it.

75 Kinsley, James. "John Dryden," English Poetry: Selected Bibliographical Guides. Edited by A. E. Dyson. New York and London: Oxford University Press, 1971. Pp. 111-27.

An essay on Dryden concluding with a checklist.

76 Love, Harold, and Mary Lord, comps. John Dryden in Australian Libraries: A Checklist of pre-1800 Holdings. (Monash University English Department Bibliographical Checklists, 1.) Melbourne: Monash University, English Department, 1972. 31 leaves. (Bibliography, leaves 3-4.)

77 Monk, Samuel Holt. John Dryden: A List of Critical Studies Published from 1895 to 1948. Minneapolis: University of Minnesota Press; London: Oxford University Press, 1950. vi + 52pp.

Reviewed in N&Q, CXCVI, 352; in TLS, April 6, 1951, 214; and, see #74 above.

78 Stratman, Carl J., C.S.V. "John Dryden's All for Love; Unrecorded Editions," PBSA, LVII (1963), 77-9.

15 items from 1710-1792.

79 _____, David G. Spencer, and Mary Elizabeth Devine,

eds. *Restoration and Eighteenth Century Theatre Research: A Bibliographical Guide, 1900-1968*. Carbondale: Southern Illinois University Press, 1971. 811pp.

Annotated. See #s 252-392 within. Reviewed by Geoffrey Marshall in SCN, XXXI, #18.

concordances

(See also #s 19, 480, and 495)

80   Montgomery, Guy, ed., with M. Jackman and H. S. Agoa. *Concordance to the Poetical Works of John Dryden*. Berkeley: University of California Press; Cambridge: Cambridge University Press, 1957; New York: Russell and Russell, 1967. viii + 722pp.

Based on the Noyes edition (#4 above). Reviewed in TLS, July 4, 1958, 378; by Pierre Legouis in EA, XI, 253-4; and, by James Kinsley in RES, X, 216.

81   Sherbo, Arthur. *A Computer Concordance of John Dryden's Translation of Virgil's Poetry*. 2 vols. East Lansing: Michigan State University, 1969.

Based on the Kinsley edition (#3 above).

82   _____. *Frequency Lists of John Dryden's Translations of Virgil's Poetry*. East Lansing: Michigan State University, Computer Center, 1971. 204 leaves.

textual studies

authorship

(See also #s 522-5, 869)

83   Faulkner, Thomas C. "Dryden and *Great and Weighty Considerations*: an Incorrect Attribution," SEL, XI (1971), 417-25.

Faulkner argues that the 1679 exclusion crisis pamphlet was not by Dryden. Charles E. Ward (in #120 below) said it was.

84   Obertello, Alfredo, ed. *Un Dramma Inglese Inedite del Secolo Diciassettesimo, The Lover's Stratagem, or Virtue Rewarded*. Geneve: Publicazione dell'Instituto Universitario de Magestero, 1952. clxvii + 188pp.

Obertello attributes the play (Bodleian, MS Rawlinson, poet. 18), c. 1680-5, to Dryden.

85 Purpus, Eugene R. "Some Notes on a Deistical Essay Attributed to Dryden," PQ, XXIX (1950), 347-9.

Purpus denies Dryden's or Blount's authorship of the essay signed 'A. W.' attributed to Dryden since 1745.

86 Wright, William Culver. "A New Edition of Thomas Wright's The Female Virtuoso's." Doctoral Dissertation: University of Maryland, 1968. 184pp.

Wright suggests that Dryden may have contributed to the play.

editing

87 Dearing, Vinton A. "Computer Aids to Editing the Text of Dryden," Art and Error: Modern Textual Editing. Edited and compiled by Ronald Gottesman and Scott Bennett. Bloomington and London: Indiana University Press, 1970. Pp. 254-78.

Collation program for the California Dryden, #6 above.

88 _____. "The Use of a Computer in Analyzing Dryden's Spelling," Literary Data Processing Conference Proceedings. New York: Modern Language Association, 1964. Pp. 200-10.

i.e., to help arrive at a copy-text and to determine the texts with the more characteristic Dryden-spellings.

89 Falle, George. "Sir Walter Scott as Editor of Dryden and Swift," UTQ, XXXVI (1967), 161-80.

Falle's analyses show that Scott's edition of Dryden is better than his Swift.

90 MacMillan, Dougald. "Clark Edition of Dryden--the Plays," SAB, May, 1949, 10-11.

Discusses the genesis and organization of the California Dryden, #6 above.

91 Roper, Alan, and J. Max Patrick. The Editor as Critic and the Critic as Editor. (Papers Read at a Clark Library Seminar, November 13, 1971.) Los Angeles: William Andrews Clark Memorial Library, University of California,

1973. vi + 78pp.

Roper discusses editing Dryden's translation of Maimbourg's Histoire de la ligue.

92   Swedenberg, H. T., Jr. "Challenges to Dryden's Editor," John Dryden: Papers Read at a Clark Library Seminar, Feb. 25, 1667. Introduction by John Loftis. Los Angeles: William Andrews Clark Memorial Library, University of California, 1967. Pp. 25-40.

Reviewed by Robert Fulkenflik in SCN, XXVI, 42; and by Philip Roberts in N&Q, XVI, 115-7.

93   _____. "On Editing Dryden's Early Poems," Essays Critical and Historical Dedicated to Lily B. Campbell. Berkeley and Los Angeles: University of California Press, 1950. Pp. 73-84.

For a copy-text, Swedenberg selects "some state of the first edition" and follows its punctuation "except where a later and authoritative text has variants that are clearly and unmistakably superior."

textual criticism

94   Bowers, Fredson. "Current Theories of Copy-Text, with an Illustration from Dryden," MP, XLVIII (1950), 12-20.

Bowers discusses press variant forms obtained from his collating 6 American copies of the 1667 edition of The Indian Emperour.

95   _____. "Dryden as Laureate: the Cancel Leaf in King Arthur," TLS, April 10, 1953, 244.

The cancel leaf in the Bodleian copy states that Dryden would have remained poet laureate if he had agreed to "terms." See #112 below.

96   _____. "The First Edition of Dryden's Wild Gallant," The Library, V (June, 1950), 51-4.

Establishes the first and second editions.

97   _____. "The Pirated Quarto of Dryden's State of Innocence," SB, V (1952-3), 166-9.

Examines the reasons why Q9 may have drawn its text from Q8 though imitating the appearance of Q4 and the variants involving Qs 4 and 9.

98 _____. "The 1665 Manuscript of Dryden's *Indian Emperour*," SP, XLVIII (1951), 738-60.

Probably, the 1665 ms is copied from the 1665 Herringman transcript and not from Dryden's foul papers.

99 _____. "Variants in Early Editions of Dryden's Plays," HLB, III (1949), 277-88.

Additions and corrections to existing descriptions.

100 Cameron, W. J. "An Overlooked Dryden Printing," N&Q, CXCVIII (1953), 334.

A 1697 imprint of *A Letter to Sir George Etherege*.

101 Caracciolo, Peter. "Some Unrecorded Variants in the First Edition of Dryden's *All for Love*, 1678," BC, XIII (1964), 498-500.

Notes the following variant reading of B2, line 23: "Who Lord it o'er Mankind, should perish, here."

102 Crinò, Anna Maria. "Dryden MS," TLS, Sept. 22, 1966, 879.

Reports of discovering a manuscript of *Heroique Stanzas on the Death of Cromwell* in the British Museum.

103 _____. "Uno Sconosciuto Autografo Drydeniana al British Museum," English Miscellany, XVII (1967), 311-20.

An essay on *Heroique Stanzas* together with the text she discovered in the British Museum.

104 Dearing, Vinton A. "Dryden's *MacFlecknoe*: the Case for Authorial Revision," SB, VII (1954), 85-102.

Suggests a relationship for the 7 mss and 2 imprints collated by Evans (#106 below).

105 Dunkin, Paul S. "The Dryden *Troilus and Cressida* Imprint: Another Theory," Publications of the Bibliographical Society of the University of Virginia, II (1949), 185-9.

Dunkin offers two hypothetical schedules: Tonson or Abel Swall published it first.

106 Evans, G. Blakemore. "The Text of Dryden's *MacFlecknoe*,"

Evans collates 7 mss, and imprints of 1682 and 1684.

107 Hamilton, Marion H. "The Early Editions of Dryden's
State of Innocence," SB, V (1952), 163-6.

Macdonald 81a, b, e, d, f, g, j, h, c is the order she
establishes (see #71 above).

108 _____. "The Manuscripts of Dryden's The State of Innocence and the Relation of the Harvard MS to the First
Quarto," SB, VI (1954), 237-46.

The Harvard ms has corrections written by Dryden.

109 Metzdorf, Robert F. "Three States of The Revolter," PBSA,
XLV (1951), 362.

The Revolter: a Tragi-Comedy Acted Between The Hind and
the Panther and Religio Laici. London, 1687. Metzdorf
says that "Revoltex" in the title of the Yale copy makes
it a first state; a second state is at the Harvard College Library; and, Macdonald 242 is a third state (see
#71 above).

110 Smith, John H. "Dryden's Prologue and Epilogue to Mithridates Revived," PMLA, LXVIII (1953), 251-67.

Smith uses the poems to show that better texts for the
prologues and epilogues are needed.

111 Steck, James. "Dryden's Indian Emperour; the Early Editions and their Relation to the Text," SB, II (1949),
139-52.

Steck supplements Macdonald and Osborn (see #71 above)
and states that Macdonald 69k was the copy-text for the
1701 Dryden folio.

112 Young, Kenneth. "Dryden as Laureate," TLS, May 8, 1953,
301.

Letter responding to #95 above. Dryden may have lost
the laureateship for political, not religious, reasons.

II BIOGRAPHY:

General Studies

113 Birrell, T. A. "John Dryden's Purchases at Two Book Auctions, 1680 and 1682," ES, XLII (1961), 193-217.

146 books, mainly on theological subjects, may have been
purchased by the poet at the Digby sale, April 19, 1680,

and the Richard Smith sale, May 15, 1682.

114   Kreissman, Bernard, ed. The <u>Life</u> <u>of</u> <u>John</u> <u>Dryden</u> <u>by</u> <u>Sir</u> <u>Walter</u> <u>Scott</u>. Lincoln: University of Nebraska Press, 1963. xx + 471pp.

      Notes, 455-64. A large-print reproduction of the 1834 text.

115   M., P. D. "John Dryden's Widow," N&Q, I (1954), 272.

      A query concerning Elizabeth Dryden's residence in Sherrard Street draws the reply from J. B. Whitmore and Wilfred H. Holden (Aug., 1954, 363) that it is now Sherwood St. in the Parish of St. James, Piccadilly.

116   Mundy, P. D. "Dryden Baronetcy (Extinct 1770)--additions to 'G.E.C.'" N&Q, CXCVIII (1953), 435-6.

      Mundy discusses (1) the third wife of Sir John Dryden, 2d Bart., (2) the mother of Sir John Dryden, 4th Bart., (3) the wife of Sir John Dryden, 4th Bart., and (4) Edward Lucke.

117   Osborn, James M. <u>John</u> <u>Dryden</u>: <u>Some</u> <u>Biographical</u> <u>Facts</u> <u>and</u> <u>Problems</u>. Revised edition. Gainesville: University of Florida Press, 1965. xlvii + 482pp.

      Reviewed by James Kinsley in ES, XLVII, 482; and by Philip Roberts in N&Q, XIV, 239-40.

118   _____. "A Lost Portrait of John Dryden," HLQ, XXXVI (1973), 341-5.

      The Baginton Hall portrait by John Riley, referred to in <u>The</u> <u>Laurel</u>, 1685, is reproduced here.

119   Ward, Charles E. "Challenges to Dryden's Biographer," <u>John</u> <u>Dryden</u>: <u>Papers</u> <u>Read</u> <u>at</u> <u>a</u> <u>Clark</u> <u>Library</u> <u>Seminar,</u> <u>Feb.</u> <u>25, 1967.</u> Introduction by John Loftis. Los Angeles: William Andrews Clark Memorial Library, University of California, 1967. Pp. 3-21.

      Reviewed as in #92 above.

120   _____. <u>The</u> <u>Life</u> <u>of</u> <u>John</u> <u>Dryden</u>. Chapel Hill: The University of North Carolina Press, 1961. x + 380pp.

      The standard biography. Reviewed by Aubrey Williams in Yale Review, LI, 617-18; by Bonamy Dobrée in The Listener, LXVIII, 292; in TLS, Sept. 14, 1962, 688; by Vivian de Sola Pinto in MLR, LVIII, 408-11; and, by James Kinsley in RES, XV, 86-8.

121 Wasserman, George R. John Dryden. (Twayne's English Authors.) New York: Twayne Publishers, Inc., 1964. 174pp.

A critical study of Dryden's life and works.

122 Young, Kenneth. John Dryden: a Critical Biography. London: Sylvan Press, 1954; New York: Russell and Russell, 1969. xvi + 240pp.

Psychoanalytic touches. Reviewed by Vivian de Sola Pinto in English, X, 190-2; in TLS, Feb. 4, 1955, 74; and, by Pierre Legouis in EA, IX, 57-8.

Literary Relationships

(See also #s 179, 313, 388, 391, 400, 409, 412-3, 422, 427, 439, 453, 455, 460-1, 464, 521-6, 542-4, 665-6, 705, 719, 752, 848, 851, 853, 864, 869, 872, 874, 878-9, 916, 953, 963, and 971)

123 Albaugh, Richard M. "Dryden's Literary Relationships, 1689-1700." Doctoral Dissertation: The Ohio State University, 1948. 116pp.

Not in Monk (#77 above); 195a in Keast (#74 above). Cited here as a rare because comprehensive treatment of the topic.

124 Archer, Stanley. "John Dryden and the Earl of Dorset," Doctoral Dissertation: University of Mississippi, 1965. 265pp.

Archer states, "the relationship was chiefly one of poet and patron. Although both men had interest in literary criticism, rhyme in drama, reform of language, and satire, neither seems to have had any appreciable influence on the other."

125 ———. "Two Dryden Anecdotes," N&Q, XX (1973), 177-8.

Discusses a visit to Dorset's estate by Dryden and Tom Brown, and the generosity of Dorset to writers.

126 Cameron, W. J. "John Dryden and Henry Hevingham," N&Q, IV (1957), 199-203.

Discusses the anonymous lampoon, A Dialogue between the Poet Motteux and Patron Heveningham, 1698, and attributes The Fair Stranger to Heveningham.

127 Johnson, Maurice. "A Literary Chestnut: Dryden's 'Cousin' Swift," PMLA, LXVII (1952), 1024-34.

Shows how "two centuries have treated the judgement on Swift attributed to Dryden," which Johnson believes apocryphal.

128 Maurer, A. E. Wallace. "Dryden's Bad Memory and a Narrow Escape," N&Q, V (1958), 212-3.

Discusses Lord Herbert's The History of Henry VIII in the context of the Dryden-Stillingfleet argument.

129 _____. "Dryden's Memory Vindicated: Proceed with Bibliographical Caution," N&Q, XIV (1967), 345-6.

Information supplementing #128 above.

130 Moore, John Robert, and Maurice Johnson. "Dryden's 'Cousin' Swift," PMLA, LXVIII (1953), 1232-40.

Swift's contempt for Dryden and his admirers was widely known and was responsible for making credible the anecdote of Dryden's pronouncement upon his poetic disability.

131 Oliver, H. J. Sir Robert Howard (1626-1698): a Critical Biography. Durham: Duke University Press, 1963. 346pp.

Treats The Indian Queen and other Dryden-Howard topics.

132 Pinto, Vivian de Sola. "Rochester and Dryden," NRMS, V (1961), 29-48.

Holds that "the impact of Rochester's personality and poetry was an important factor in Dryden's development."

133 Smith, John H. "Dryden and Buckingham: the Beginnings of the Feud," MLN, LXIX (1954), 242-5.

Traces the antipathy to 1667.

134 Turner, W. Arthur. "Milton, Marvell, and 'Dradon' at Cromwell's Funeral," PQ, XXVIII (1949), 320-3.

Documents the presence of the three ('Dradon' = Dryden) at the funeral.

Religion

(see also #s 113, 148, 724-9, 732, 735, 748-49, 751, 753, 755, 757, 759, 761-3, and 765)

135 Archer, Stanley. "A Dryden Record," N&Q, XIII (1966), 264-5.

An English Army Lists note concerning Catholic proponents of the King may refer to Dryden's son.

136 Benson, Donald R. "John Dryden and The Church of England: the Conversion and the Problem of Authority in the Seventeenth Century." Doctoral Dissertation: University of Kansas, 1959. 384pp.

Holds that Dryden became a Catholic because "only an assertion of spiritual infallibility against the private spirit in religion could preserve the nation from political chaos, and consequently spiritual destruction, and the Anglican Church would not make such an assertion."

137 _____. "Theology and Politics in Dryden's Conversion," SEL, IV (1964), 393-412.

Benson argues that for Dryden "controversial religious questions had to be authoritatively settled" because they were closely tied to political stability.

138 Birrell, T. A. "James Maurus Corker and Dryden's Conversion," ES, LIV (1973), 461-9.

Discusses the English Benedictine monk who received Dryden into the Catholic Church, and notes the order's "impeccable loyalty to the Stuart cause."

139 Mundy, P. D. "Dryden's Dominican Son--Sir Erasmus Henry Dryden, 5th Bart." N&Q, CXCVI (1951), 472-3.

Attempts to correct "errors" in a June, 1951 issue of Blackfriars.

140 Sweney, John R. "The Religion of Lady Elizabeth Howard Dryden," N&Q, XIX (1972), 365.

States that she had been a Catholic long before Dryden's conversion.

III COMPREHENSIVE OR MISCELLANEOUS STUDIES:

141 Amarasinghe, Upali. Dryden and Pope in the Early Nineteenth Century: a Study of Changing Literary Taste, 1800-1830. Cambridge: Cambridge University Press, 1962. 244pp.

Reviewed in TLS, Feb. 1, 1963, 78; by G. D. Klingopulos in MLR, LVIII, 245-6; by John Colmer in Southern Review, I, 95-7; and, by E. R. Loomis in ANQ, I, 126-7.

142 Atkins, George Douglas. "Dryden and the Clergy," Doctoral Dissertation: University of Virginia, 1969. 228pp.

Examines the plays and political poems and notes a significant approval of priests.

143 Buhtz, Georg. "Drydens moralische Gedankenwelt." Doctor-Dissertation: Universität Hamburg, 1958. 283pp.

144 Calder-Marshall, Arthur. "Dryden and the Rise of Modern Publishing," History Today, Sept., 1952, 641-5.

In the context of an age of patronage.

145 Cope, Jackson I. "Dryden vs Hobbes: an Adaptation from the Platonists," JEGP, LVII (1958), 444-8.

The poet's rejection of "philosophic materialism" and "aesthetic naturalism."

146 Crinò, Anna Maria. John Dryden. (Biblioteca dell'Archivum Romanicum, I, 50.) Firenze: L. S. Olschki, 1957. 406pp.

Bibliography, 753-83. Reviewed by John Killham in MLR, LIII, 460-1; by James Kinsley in RES, IX, 452; and, by Jackson I. Cope in MLN, LXXIV, 636-40.

147 ──────. "Ritorno al Dryden," Cultura e Scuola, I (1962), 65-71.

A brief summary of major critical assessments of Dryden from Alexander Pope to Mario Praz (with emphasis on the Italians).

148 Dobrée, Bonamy. John Dryden. (Writers and Their Work, 70.) New York and London: Longmans, Green, 1956. 48pp.

Published for the British Council and National Book League. Reviewed by Pierre Legouis in EA, X, 258.

149 Faulkner, Susan Newlander. "The Concept of Decorum in Dryden's Works." Doctoral Dissertation: The City University of New York, 1973. 256pp.

Faulkner writes, "His approach to decorum--or propriety--was characterized by a tension between his realization of the need to follow the received precepts and his desire to express his individual creative impulses."

150 Gardner, William Bradford. "John Dryden's Interest in Judicial Astrology," SP, XLVII (1950), 506-21.

Gardner sees four categories: serious, satirical, humorous, and embellishment.

151 Guzzetti, Alfred Felix. "Dryden's Two Worlds: Restoration Society and the Literary Past." Doctoral Dissertation: Harvard University, 1968. 173pp.

152 Hoffman, Arthur W. "Some Aspects of Dryden's Imagery." Doctoral Dissertation: Yale University, 1951. 184pp.

153 _____. John Dryden's Imagery. Gainesville: University of Florida Press, 1962. 172pp.

Emphasizes theological, political, and literary imagery. Pp. 1-19 reprinted in #156 below as "An Apprenticeship in Praise"; 130-47 reprinted in #172 below as "Various John Dryden: 'All, All, of a piece Throughout.'" Reviewed by Arthur Sherbo in Criticism, V, 379-82; by B. Robie in ANQ, I, 127-8; Bernard Schilling in JEGP, LXIII, 362-4; by James McPhee in N&Q, XI, 117-19; and, by John Carey in RES, XV, 432-3.

154 Horn, András. "Gedanken über Rationalitat und Illusion: Apropos John Dryden," Festschrift Rudolf Stamm. Edited by Eduard Kolb and Jörg Hasler. Bern: Franke, 1969. Pp. 189-201.

155 Horsman, E. A. "Dryden's French Borrowings," RES, I (1950), 346-51.

Substantiates Samuel Johnson's charge that Dryden showed off his French.

156 King, Bruce, ed. Dryden's Mind and Art. Edinburgh: Oliver & Boyd, 1969; New York: Barnes & Noble, Inc., 1970. x + 213pp.

Bibliography, 206-13. Contains King's essay, "Absalom and Achitophel: a Revaluation," 65-83, and nine other essays old and new by various hands: see #s 259, 514, 571, 645, 667, 749, and 962. In his essay King sees the poem as an "anatomy" satirizing a cast of mind.

157 _____. Twentieth Century Interpretations of All for Love. (Twentieth Century Interpretations.) Englewood Cliffs: Prentice-Hall, Inc., 1968. viii + 120pp.

Introduction, 1-13, on the background and elements of the play. Reprinted essays by various hands. See #s 174, 201, 266, 277, 306, 308, 312, 315, and 333 below.

158 Kinsley, James and Helen, eds. Dryden: the Critical Heritage. (The Critical Heritage Series.) New York: Barnes & Noble, Inc.; London: Routledge & Kegan Paul, Ltd., 1971. x + 414pp.

Critical assessments of Dryden's work. The essays date from 1663 to 1810. Reviewed in TLS, Nov. 26, 1971, 1472.

159 Lees, F. N. "John Dryden," The Pelican Guide to English Literature. Vol. IV: From Dryden to Johnson. Baltimore and Harmondsworth: Penguin Books, Inc., 1957. Pp. 97-113.

160 Link, Frederick M. "A Decade of Dryden Scholarship," PLL, VIII (1972), 427-43. (Review essay.)

161 Love, Harold. "The Satirized Characters in Poeta De Tristibus," PQ, XLVII (1968), 547-62.

Discusses the portrait of Dryden in the second canto of the anonymous 1682 poem.

162 McHenry, Robert, and David Lougee, eds. Critics on Dryden. (Readings in Literary Criticism.) London: George Allen and Unwin, Ltd., 1973.

163 Maurer, A. E. Wallace. "Dryden's Knowledge of Historians, Ancient and Modern," N&Q, VI (1959), 264-6.

Examines Dryden's "interests in and uses of" Herodian, Eusebius, Guicciardine, Knowles, and others.

164 _____. "Dryden's View of History." Doctoral Dissertation: University of Wisconsin, 1954. 185pp.

165 Meadows, A. J. The High Firmament: a Survey of Astronomy in English Literature. Leicester: Leicester University Press, 1969. x + 207pp.

Scattered notes on Dryden's use of astrology.

166 Miner, Earl. The Restoration Mode from Milton to Dryden. Princeton: Princeton University Press, 1974. Pp. 288-

367, 508-40.

Comprehensive essays with a preface dated 1972.

167 _____, ed. John Dryden. (Writers and Their Background.) Athens: Ohio University Press; London: G. Bell & Sons, Ltd., 1972. xxvi + 363pp.

Chronology, xiii-xxvi; bibliography, 325-47. Miner's "On Reading Dryden," 1-26, essays the poet's reputation, works, and literary milieu. All new articles: see #s 215, 232, 258, 573, 610, 689, 782, 827, and 961 below.

168 Myers, William. Dryden. London: Hutchinson & Co., Ltd., 1973. 200pp.

Bibliography, 193-4. Ten chapters develop Myer's argument that Dryden "learned to deploy a limited and perhaps debased poetic idiom in an examination of the human problems created by the pressures of history."

169 Murray, Byron D. "Lowell's Criticism of Dryden and Pope." Doctoral Dissertation: University of Iowa, 1953.

170 Parra, Antonio R. "Considerazioni sulla Fortuna di John Dryden nell' Italia del Settecento," RLMC, XX (1969), 1746.

171 Raine, Kathleen. "A Dryden Quotation," TLS, Sept. 13, 1957, 547.

Query concerning Blake's use of a quote attributed to Dryden by Rossetti (?): "At length for hatching ripe he breaks the shell," title, pl. 6, Gates of Paradise.

172 Schilling, Bernard, ed. Dryden: a Collection of Critical Essays. (Twentieth Century Views.) Englewood Cliffs: Prentice-Hall, Inc., 1963. vi + 186pp.

Chronology, 182-5; bibliography, 186. Introduction, 1-7, surveys the reprinted essays contained in this collection. See #s 15 (introduction reprinted here as "On the Poetics of Terminal Tragedy: Dryden's All for Love"), 153, 193, 610, 663, 675, 758, and 833.

173 St. John, L. "Dryden's Political Tone." Doctoral Dissertation: The University of Alberta, 1972. 213pp.

174 Smith, David Nichol. John Dryden. (The Clark Lectures on English Literature, 1948-9.) London and New York: Cambridge University Press, 1950; Folcroft, Pa.: Folcroft Press, 1969. 92pp.

Four lectures: (1) Early Verse and Criticism, (2) Plays (portions reprinted in #157 above), (3) Satires and Religious Poems, and (4) Translations, Odes, and Fables. Reviewed by H. Kossmann in ES, XXXII, 40; by Charles E. Ward in MLN, LXVII, 489-90; and, in TLS, Mar. 24, 1950, 186.

175 Sutherland, James R. English Literature of the Late Seventeenth Century. New York and Oxford: Oxford University Press, 1969. vii + 589pp.

Comprehensive essays on Dryden.

176 _____. "John Dryden," The New Encyclopaedia Britannica. 15th edition. Macropaedia, vol. V, 1062-5.

177 Swedenberg, H. T., Jr., ed. Essential Articles for the Study of John Dryden. (The Essential Articles Series.) London: Frank Cass & Co., Ltd.; Hamden, Conn.: Archon Books, 1966. xvi + 587pp.

Bibliography, 586-7. Reprinted articles by various hands. See #s 297, 534, 572, 600, 690, 749, 758, 867. Reviewed by Pierre Legouis, EA, XX, 439-40.

178 Sweney, John Robert. "Political Attacks on Dryden, 1681-1683." Doctoral Dissertation: The University of Wisconsin, 1968. 260pp.

He writes, "The study examines the attacks, and to some extent Dryden's replies to his critics (in The Medal, The Second Part of Absalom and Achitophel, The Duke of Guise, and The Vindication of the Duke of Guise) from the standpoint of political rhetoric, designed to bolster the morale of party adherents and to sway the large and crucially important numbers of uncommitted readers."

179 Wallace, A. E. "Dryden and Pyrrhonism," N&Q, IV (1957), 251-2.

A passage from Dryden's Life of Plutarch supports the argument that he sought to set up objective standards for judgements and sought certainty in his reasoning.

180 Welle, Jojakim Adriaan Van Der. Dryden and Holland. Groningen: J. B. Wolters, 1962. vii + 153pp.

Examines Dryden's attitude toward Holland; treats Amboyna only briefly. Reviewed in TLS, Jan. 23, 1964, 69.

181 Williams, David. "Dryden and Donne: a Study in Literary Relationship." Doctoral Dissertation: Yale University, 1972.

182 Young, Donald Leroy. "The Reputation of John Dryden, 1895-1956." Doctoral Dissertation: Boston University, 1960. 659pp.

IV DRAMA: (SEE ALSO #776)

  Comprehensive and Miscellaneous Subjects

183 Archer, Stanley L. "Some Early References to Dryden," N&Q, XVII (1970), 417-18.

  He illustrates Dryden's prestige as a critic and dramatist.

184 Arnold, Claude. "Reflections of Political Issues in the Plays, Prologues, and Epilogues of John Dryden." Doctoral Dissertation: The Case Western Reserve University, 1958.

185 Bevan, Allan R. "Dryden as a Dramatic Artist." Doctoral Dissertation: University of Toronto, 1953. 345pp.

186 Brown, F. Andrew. "Shakespeare in Germany: Dryden, Langbaine, and the 'Acta Eruditorum,'" The Germanic Review, XL (1965), 86-95.

  Discusses the Dryden-Langbaine controversy's influence on the philological journal begun in Germany in 1682.

187 Davenport, Warren W. "Private and Social Order in the Drama of John Dryden." Doctoral Dissertation: University of Florida, 1970. 225pp.

188 Erlich, Richard D., and James Harner. "Pope's Annotations in his Copy of Dryden's Comedies, Tragedies, and Operas: an Exercise in Cryptography," RECTR, X (May, 1971), 14-24.

  The conclusion is that "versification was the main criterion for Pope's selection of the majority of his marked lines." With Harner's collation for Pope's volumes.

189 Forrester, Kent Allen. "Supernaturalism in Restoration Drama." Doctoral Dissertation: University of Utah, 1971. 191pp.

  Examines The Tempest, The Rehearsal, and The Duke of Guise for the political implications of supernaturalism. Concludes that "the clash between the Restoration climate of opinion and the more deeply-rooted beliefs in the non-Christian supernatural resulted, for the most part, in plays that seem flawed in conception and execution."

190 Gohn, Ernest S. "Seventeenth-Century Theories of the Passions and the Plays of John Dryden." Doctoral Dissertation: The Johns Hopkins University, 1948.

Not in Monk (#77 above); 433a in Keast (#74 above). Cited here as a rare because comprehensive treatment of the topic.

191 Hughes, Leo. The Drama's Patrons: a Study of the Eighteenth-Century London Audiences. Austin and London: University of Texas Press, 1971. Pp. 90-4.

Concludes that Dryden "commonly rests his case on the cultivated tastes of the few."

192 Irie, Keitaro. "The Auxiliary 'Do' in John Dryden's Plays," Anglica, V (1962), 1-19.

193 Izume, Kenji. "Probleme der Aufführung Shakespeares in Japan," SJ, XCIX (1963) 133-41.

194 Kaul, R. K. "Rhyme and Blank Verse in Drama: a Note on Eliot," English, XV (1964), 96-9.

Links Dryden, Addison, and Samuel Johnson with T. S. Eliot.

195 King, Bruce. Dryden's Major Plays. Edinburgh: Oliver & Boyd, Ltd.; New York: Barnes & Noble, Inc., 1966. x + 215pp.

The premise is that "the heroic plays have been badly misinterpreted for almost two centuries, and because of this Dryden's later work has been seen in a wrong perspective." King believes that "All for Love has an undeserved reputation while Don Sebastian and Marriage a la Mode have been neglected." Reviewed by Wm. Myers in RES, XVIII, 334-6; by Eugene M. Waith in Yale Review, LVII, 123-6; and, Paul E. Parnell in RECTR, VII (Nov. 1967), 56-9.

196 _____. "Dryden's Treatment of Ideas and Themes in his Dramatic Works, with Some Reference to the Intellectual Movements of his Time." Doctoral Dissertation: Leeds University, 1960.

197 Larson, Richard Leslie. "Studies in Dryden's Dramatic Technique: the Use of Scenes Depicting Persuasion and Accusation." Doctoral Dissertation: Harvard Universi-

ty, 1963.

198 Lehman, Elmar. "'If the People Have the Power': Zum Motiv des Volksaufenlandes im Drama John Drydens," Poetica, IV (1971), 437-61.

A study in the history of ideas dealing solely with the dramas from The Indian Queen to Cleomenes.

199 Lill, James Vernon. "Dryden's Adaptations from Milton, Shakespeare, and Chaucer." Doctoral Dissertation: The University of Minnesota, 1954. 284pp.

Argues that "Dryden's constant endeavor was to define standards, by means of which English poetry might move forward with the other arts and sciences, and to compose in the enlightened mode of these standards," and, therefore, Dryden adapts other works to the Restoration idiom.

200 McFadden, George. "Dryden and the Numbers of His Native Tongue," Essays and Studies in Language and Literature. (Duquesne Studies, Philological Series, 5.) Herbert H. Petit, general editor. Pittsburgh: Duquesne University Press, 1964. Pp. 87-109.

By 'numbers' he means the "auditory imagination," which is the "interpenetration of a poet's vision of the world with the stock of words, phrases, cadences, chosen in great part for their sound, which are characteristic of his way of putting that world before the reader."

201 Merchant, W. Moelwyn. "Shakespeare 'Made Fit,'" Restoration Theatre. Edited by John Russell Brown and Bernard Harris. London: Edward Arnold (Publishers), Ltd., 1965; New York: Capricorn Books, 1967. Pp. 195-214.

Examines The Tempest, All for Love, and Troilus and Cressida, whose preface is a "convenient epitome" of Restoration principles of adapting Shakespeare.

202 Milosevitch, Vincent M. "Propriety as an Esthetic Principle in Dryden, Shakespeare, and Wagner," HAB, XXI, (1970), 3-13.

203 Moore, John Robert. "Political Allusions in Dryden's Later Plays," PMLA, LXXIII (1958), 36-42.

Moore examines Dryden's political views from 1689+ and finds boldness and honesty.

204 Olinder, Britta. "Acts and Scenes in John Dryden's Theory and Practice." Doctoral Dissertation: Universitet Göteborg, 1971

205 Payne, Rhoda. "Stage Direction during the Restoration," TA, XX (1963), 41-63.

Traces the rise in importance of the director in a discussion of Dryden, Davenant, Betterton and others. Illustrated.

206 Sánchez Escribano, Federico. "Lope de Vega según una alusión de John Dryden," El Hispano (Albuquerque, N. M.), XVI, 101-2.

207 Scharf, Gerhard. Charaktergestaltung und psychologischer Gehalt, in Drydens Shakespeare-Bearbeitungen. (Hamburger Philologische Studien.) Hamburg: H. Buske, 1970. 147pp. (Bibliography, 133-44.)

208 Shaheen, Abdel-Rahman Abdel Kader. "Satiric Characterization in John Dryden's Later Works." Doctoral Dissertation: University of Houston, 1972. 294pp.

Argues that Dryden's "Use of the Theophrastan tradition of Character-writing and of the rhetorical tradition affected his conception of satire and character, and in practice shaped his allusive method of satiric characterization in the dramatic and non-dramatic works."

209 Singh, Sarup. The Theory of Drama in the Restoration Period. Bombay: Orient Longmans, 1963. xii + 299pp.

210 Stroup, Thomas Bradley. Type-Characters in the Serious Drama of the Restoration with Special Attention to the Plays of Davenant, Dryden, Lee, and Otway. (Kentucky Microcards, Series A, 5.) Lexington: University of Kentucky, 1956.

211 Tritt, Carleton Stephen. "Wit and Paradox in Dryden's Serious Plays." Doctoral Dissertation: University of Washington, 1968. 251pp.

A study in the history of ideas noting that Dryden's use of the concepts passes from a noncommitted position through "fanciful, sentimental, ethical, satiric, and finally tragic wit."

212 Visser, Colin Wills. "Dryden's Plays: a Critical Assessment." Doctoral Dissertation: University of Rochester, 1968. 419pp.

The comedies exhibit a "balance between romantic and satiric elements"; the tragedies are "not didactic but affective. They do not objectify a moral system; their value lies in the quality of the emotional response they provoke in the spectator."

213 von Lengefeld, Wilhelm Freiherr Kleinschmidt. "Ist Shakespeares Stil barok? Bemerkungen zur Sprache Shakespeares und Drydens," <u>Shakespeare Studien</u>: <u>Festschrift für Heinrich Mutschmann</u>; <u>zum 65 Geburtstag</u>. Überreicht von den Herausgebern Walter Fischer und Karl Wentersdorf. Marburg: Elwert, 1951. Pp. 88-106.

214 Wahba, Magdi, and Muhammed Muhammed Ināni. Dráydan wa-al-shi'r al-masrahl. Cairo: Dar al Mahraf, 1964. 209pp.

    Arabic title, transliterated as above (<u>Dryden</u> and <u>Poetic Drama</u>).

215 Waith, Eugene M. "Dryden and the Tradition of Serious Drama," in #167 above, pp. 58-89.

    Waith traces the development of the epic hero and Drydens portrayals, noting that "they are all extraordinary personages, possessed of that special fortitude, or <u>arete</u>, which distinguishes the heroes of ancient epic."

216 Weinbrot, Howard D. "Robert Gould: Some Borrowings from Dryden," ELN, III (1965), 36-40..

    Illustrates that Gould's <u>The Playhouse</u> was influenced by <u>All for Love</u>, <u>The Conquest of Granada</u>, and <u>Of Dramatic Poesy</u>, <u>an Essay</u>.

217 West, Michael. "Dryden and the Disintegration of Renaissance Heroic Ideals," Costerus, VII (1973), 193-22.

    West concludes that "the entire progression of Dryden's dramas is perhaps best explained as the final stage in the decay of Renaissance ideals of Christian heroism."

218 Zamonski, John A. "Redemptive Love in the Plays of John Dryden: from <u>Wild Gallant</u> to <u>All for Love</u>." Doctoral Dissertation: Ohio University, 1970. 191pp.

    The purpose of this study is to trace the development of Dryden's concept of Redemptive Love, which reaches its full definition in <u>All for Love</u>. In that play Love is an agent-force which (1) transcends the temporal world, (2) manifests itself through the conjugal love relationship, (3) is not controlled by reason, and (4) rewards those lovers whose fidelity is authentic. Each of the plays contributes to the development of the concept.

On the Prologues and Epilogues

219 Castrop, Helmut. "Die Satire in Drydens Prologen und Epi-

logen," Archiv, CCVIII (1972), 267-85.

220 Danchin, Pierre. "Le public des théâtres londoniens à l'époque de la Restauration d'àpres les prologues et les épilogues," <u>Dramaturgie et Société: Rapports entre l'oeuvre théâtrale</u>. Edité par Jean Jacquot, et al. 2 vols. Paris, 1968. II, 847-88.

221 Sutherland, James. "Prologues, Epilogues and Audience in the Restoration Theatre," <u>Of Books and Humankind: Essays and Poems Presented to Bonamy Dobrée</u>. Edited by John Butt, et al. London: Routledge & Kegan Paul, Ltd., 1964. Pp. 37-54.

   Notes the subjects of these poems and the convention of singling out groups in the audience for direct address.

222 Vieth, David M. "The Art of the Prologue and Epilogue: a New Approach Based on Dryden's Practice," Genre, V (1972), 271-92.

   Vieth argues that the poems must be examined as parts of the plays and independently, and focusses on Dryden's exploitation of the speaker as actor and satirist.

223 Zwicker, Steven N. "Dryden's Borrowing from Ben Jonson's 'Panegyre.'" N&Q, XV (1968), 105-6.

   The last line of Dryden's prologue to John Bank's <u>The Unhappy Favorite</u> comes from line 162 of Jonson's poem.

On the Comedies

224 Blackwell, Herbert Robinson. "Some Formulary Characteristics of John Dryden's Comedies." Doctoral Dissertation: University of Virginia, 1967. 323pp.

   Examines characterization, rhetoric, farce, and stage conventions.

225 Bode, Robert F. "A Study of the Development of the Theme of Love and Duty in English Comedy from Charles I to George I." Doctoral Dissertation: University of South Carolina, 1970. 149pp.

   Bode states, "This study deals with the inception of the particular version of the Theme of Love and Honor . . . and the development of that theme into the Theme of Love and Duty toward the end of the seventeenth century."

226 Brewer, Gwendolyn Whitehead. "The Course of Mirth: Satiric Imagery in Selected Comedies of John Dryden." Doctoral Dissertation: Claremont Graduate School and University Center, 1968. 228pp.

The Wild Gallant, Marriage à la Mode, The Kind Keeper, and Amphitryon.

227 Davis, Floyd Herman, Jr. "The Dramaturgical Function of Song, Dance, and Music in the Comedies of John Dryden." Doctoral Dissertation: Ball State University, 1972. 202pp.

Davis "analyzes Dryden's dramaturgical use of or reference to song, dance, and music as they contribute to plot, character and setting," and speculates along these lines on the rest of the dramatic canon.

228 Deitz, Jonathan Eric. "The Design of Plot: the New Direction in Plot Resolution of the Late Restoration Satiric Comedy." Doctoral Dissertation: University of Pennsylvania, 1972. 242pp.

Deitz examines the plotting of the individual characters.

229 Fujimura, Thomas H. The Restoration Comedy of Wit. Princeton: Princeton University Press, 1952; New York: Barnes & Noble, Inc., 1968. viii + 232.

Illustrates the differences between "intrinsic" and "peripheral" meanings in the comedies of the period, with an emphasis on Dryden's plays and criticism.

230 Grace, John William. "Theory and Practice in the Comedy of John Dryden." Doctoral Dissertation: The University of Michigan, 1957.

Grace applies Dryden's critical terms to the plays.

231 Hume, R. D. "Theory of Comedy in the Restoration," MP, LXX (1973), 302-18.

The Dryden-Shadwell controversy and the comedy of wit, humour, and satire.

232 Loftis, John. "Dryden's Comedies," in #167 above, Pp. 27-57.

Essays Dryden's achievement and its historical contexts.

233 _____. "The Hispanic Element in Dryden," EUQ, XX (1964), 90-100.

Summarizes previous studies and discusses Calderón, Lope de Vega, and Camoens, noting the closeness of the Spanish and English stages.

234 _____. The Spanish Plays of Neoclassical England. New Haven and London: Yale University Press, 1973. Pp. 97-130.

In chapter four, "Dryden and Wycherley: Spanish Plot to Comedy of Manners," Loftis concludes that "Dryden remained on the middle ground of Fletcherian romance and Jonsonian comedy of humours."

235 Love, Harold. "Dryden, D'urfey, and the Standard of Comedy," SEL, XIII (1973), 422-36.

Discusses a controversy involving Dryden, D'urfey, Congreve, Guildon, and Southerne, and concludes that Dryden "can be seen moving towards a broader concept of the dulce of comedy in which the highest value is neither repartee nor plot, but 'just design' conceived as a merging of separate excellences into a harmonious, aesthetic whole."

236 McNamara, Peter Lance. "John Dryden's Contribution to the English Comic Tradition of Witty Love-Play." Doctoral Dissertation: Tulane University, 1964. 328pp.

Argues that Dryden's criticisms "taken together, form a theory of the importance of love-play to comic drama," and concludes that "Considered in conjunction with the witty debates in his plays, this theory forms an irrefutable argument for Dryden's prominence in the development of comic drama from his age" to the present.

237 Morgan, P. "Fop Art: Dryden on Comedy," ES, LIII (1972), 334-9.

States that "Dryden prized his reputation as a comic writer very highly and, to assure it, pandered to the fickle tastes of a changing audience."

238 Moore, Frank Harper. "Dryden's Theory and Practice of Comedy." Doctoral Dissertation: The University of North Carolina at Chapel Hill, 1953. 345pp.

239 _____. The Nobler Pleasure: Dryden's Comedy in Theory and Practice. Chapel Hill: The University of North Carolina Press, 1963. 264pp.

The Montague Summers text of the plays. Reviewed by A. W. Hoffman in MLQ, XXV, 498-9; by Bruce King in Sew Rev, LXXII, 543-4; by R. E. Moore in CE, XXV, 313; in

TLS, Jan. 23, 1964, 69; by W. M. Peterson in RES, XVI, 73-5; and, by Arthur C. Kirsch in MP, LXII, 255-6.

240 Muir, Kenneth. *The Comedy of Manners*. London: Hutchinson & Co., Ltd., 1970. Pp. 41-54.

The Wild Gallant, *An Evening's Love*, and *Marriage à la Mode*.

241 Schneider, Ben Ross, Jr. *The Ethos of Restoration Comedy*. Urbana, Chicago, and London: The University of Illinois Press, 1971. 201pp.

Uses Dryden's comedies as part of a study which assesses "a body of literature declaring moral instruction to be its main purpose."

242 Schwarz, Janet Lee. "A Labyrinth of Design: a Study of Dryden's Dramatic Comedy." Doctoral Dissertation: University of California at Berkeley, 1969. 237pp.

Thirteen plays "grouped by their dominant forms' and examined for their comic devices, which show Dryden "to be both conservative and inventive, recombining existing elements to create new dramatic forms."

243 Shafer, Yvonne Bonsall. "The Proviso Scene in Restoration Comedy," RECTR, IX (May, 1970), 1-10.

Examines *The Wild Gallant*, *Secret Love*, and *Amphitryon*.

244 Staves, Sarah Susan. "Studies in the Comedy of John Dryden." Doctoral Dissertation: University of Virginia, 1967. 268pp.

Staves argues that Dryden "will not give up the values and certainties of the Renaissance and earlier seventeenth century in order to commit himself to starting afresh to work out new values. Yet he is too interested in the new philosophy and the new science to let scepticism alone."

On Heroic Drama

245 Alssid, Michael William. "Dryden's Rhymed Heroic Tragedies: a Critical Study of the Plays and their Place in Dryden's Poetry." Doctoral Dissertation: Syracuse University, 1959. 442pp.

Revaluates the plays, "first, to consider carefully Dryden's effort to create a 'new' genre by fusing certain dominant characteristics of epic and tragedy, the two most celebrated Augustan literary genres; second, to examine in some detail structural and thematic features of the plays and rhetorical and metrical features of the verse; third, to suggest ways of relating these works to Dryden's non-dramatic poems."

246 Banks, Landrum. "Dryden's Baroque Drama," Essays in Honor of Esmond Linworth Marilla. Edited by Thomas Austin Kirby and William John Olive. Baton Rouge: Louisiana State University Press, 1970. Pp. 188-200.

Traces the roots of the heroic plays to Shakespeare and concludes that Dryden's drama is a "culmination rather than a foreshadowing of Neoclassicism or a protraction of the Renaissance."

247 _____. "The Imagery of Dryden's Rhymed Heroic Drama." Doctoral Dissertation: University of Tennessee, 1967. 234pp.

Finds some classical imagery used to elevate the style, but illustrates that common experiences dominate the patterns.

248 Barbeau, Anne Therese. "John Dryden's Scheme of Values: a Study of His Heroic Plays and Early Narrative Poems." Doctoral Dissertation: The City University of New York, 1968. 353pp.

Argues that "Dryden's optimistic view of history, his notion that it is moving toward an ever increasing implementation of justice, underlies both the heroic drama and the narrative poems Annus Mirabilis and Astraea Redux."

249 _____. The Intellectual Design of John Dryden's Heroic Plays. New Haven: Yale University Press, 1970. ix + 221pp.

Reviewed by Arthur Scouten in PQ, L, 422-3; by Colin Visser in UTQ, XLII, 170-5; by Eric Rothstein in JEGP, LXX, 157-61; and, by Lois Potter in ES, LIV, 391-3.

250 Bleuler, Werner. Das heroische Drama John Drydens als Experiment dekorativer Formkunst. (Swiss Studies in English, 45.) Bern: Franke, 1957. 118pp.

Reviewed by Hans Schneider in Archiv, CXCVIII, 329; and by H. Servotte in LB, LIII, 57-8.

251 Bowler, Elizabeth A. "The Augustan Heroic Idiom in Dry-

den, Rowe, and Pope." Doctoral Dissertation: University of Bristol, 1973.

252 Bradbrook, M. C. *English Dramatic Form: a History of its Development.* London: Chatto & Windus, Ltd., 1965. 205pp.

Discusses the heroic plays in chapter six, "Prisoners and Politics: the Social Image from Shakespeare to Dryden."

253 Campbell, Dowling. "Background and Applications of the Honor Code in Dryden's Four Spanish Oriented Heroic Plays." Doctoral Dissertation: University of Missouri, 1973.

254 Cope, Jackson I. "Paradise Regained: Inner Ritual," MS, I (1969), 51-65.

Discusses the rhyme-blank verse controversy and Dryden's use of 'Satan' in the heroic plays.

255 Fetrow, Fred Marion. "Dryden's Dramatic Heroes: Conception and Mode." Doctoral Dissertation: University of Nebraska, 1970. 249pp.

Concludes that, "The composite picture of the heroes in the serious drama affords a hint of Dryden's world view, which persistently suggests the need in all men of passive virtues like patience, temperance, moderation, and equanimity by exhibiting them in those characters who are more than man."

256 Fujimura, Thomas H. "The Appeal of Dryden's Heroic Plays," PMLA, LXXV (1960), 37-45.

Examines the reasons for the appeal of heroic drama, asserting that the age was sceptical and naturalistic and approved of a benign image of nature and a hero who represented the natural man.

257 Gagen, Jean. "Love and Honor in Dryden's Plays," PMLA, LXXVII (1962), 208-20.

Examines the Platonism and Renaissance humanism behind love and honor in the heroic plays.

258 Hagstrum, Jean Howard. "Dryden's Grotesque: an Aspect of the Baroque in His Art and Criticism," in #167 below, pp. 90-119.

Sees Dryden's villains as grotesque portrayals set in an antithetical context--like Maximin's.

259 Heath-Stubbs, John. "Dryden and the Heroic Ideal," in #156 above, pp. 3-23.

States that "the baroque heroic ideal represented for Dryden the realization in poetic terms of a transcendent order."

260 Huneycutt, Melicent. "The Changing Concept of the Ideal Statesman as Reflected in English Verse Drama During the Reign of Charles II: 1660-1685." Doctoral Dissertation: The University of North Carolina at Chapel Hill, 1968. 281pp.

All for Love, Aureng-Zebe, The Conquest of Granada, and The Indian Emperour.

261 Nelson, James E. "Drums and Trumpets," RECTR, IX (Nov., 1970), 46-55; X (May, 1971), 54-7.

A two-part study of battle scenes.

262 Jefferson, D. W. "'All, all of a piece throughout': Thoughts on Dryden's Dramatic Poetry," Restoration Theatre. Edited by John Russell Brown and Bernard Harris. (Stratford-Upon-Avon Studies, 6.) London: Edward Arnold (Publishers) Ltd., 1965; New York: Capricorn Books, 1967. Pp. 159-76.

Demonstrates the continuities in Dryden's heroic plays through theme and imagery.

263 _____. "Aspects of Dryden's Imagery," EIC, IV (1954), 20-41.

Holds that Dryden "reacted against metaphysical tortousness and obscurity, but he did not lose the metaphysical art of using images suggestively and wittily." Reprinted in #156 above, 24-42.

264 King, Bruce. "Heroic and Mock-Heroic Plays," Sew Rev, LXX (1962), 514-17.

Reviews Bonamy Dobree's Five Heroic Plays (New York, 1961), noting that the edition offers the "non-specialist the kind of bad serious play that Dryden's contemporaries were writing, and helps to define departures from the norm." King discusses Dryden's satire of the Heroic play.

265 Kirsch, Arthur C. "Dryden, Corneille, and the Heroic Play," MP, LIX (1962), 248-64.

Discusses gloire and Dryden's implementation of it.

266 _____. *Dryden's Heroic Drama*. Princeton: Princeton University Press, 1965; New York: Gordian Press, 1972. 157pp.

Illustrates Dryden's debts to the Jacobean and Caroline court stages, analyzing the plays' designs in a series of essays. Reviewed by Eliz. Mackenzie in RES, XVIII, 336-7; by William Frost in JEGP, LXV, 189-92; by H. Haddaway in SCN, XXIV, 2-3; by Clifford Leech in MLR, LXI, 675-7; and, by Geoffrey Bullough in English, XVI, 19-20.

267 _____. "Dryden's Theory and Practice of the Rhymed Heroic Play." Doctoral Dissertation: Princeton University, 1961. 248pp.

Examines Dryden's achievement within the traditions of Fletcher and Corneille. Three chapters on theory, two on practice.

268 Martin, Leslie H., Jr. "Conventions of the French Romances in the Drama of John Dryden." Doctoral Dissertation: Stanford University, 1967.

Martin argues that the "failure of heroic drama to remain viable arises not from the inferiority of the romances but from changes in values and ideals that resulted in the demise of both forms."

269 Molinoff, Marlene Sirota. "The Via Media of Dryden's Tragicomedy." Doctoral Dissertation: The George Washington University, 1973.

270 Newman, Robert Stanley. "The Tragedy of Wit: the Development of Heroic Drama from Dryden to Addison." Doctoral Dissertation: University of California at Los Angeles, 1964. 348pp.

Notes a similarity between Restoration comedy and heroic drama on the point of an "idealizing" couched in a "skeptical and satiric wit."

271 Osborn, Scott C. "Heroical Love in Dryden's Heroic Drama," PMLA, LXXIII (1958), 480-90.

His thesis is that "the key to Dryden's treatment of love lies in the medical and moral theories of the seventeenth century school of humours psysiology and psychology."

272 Pati, P. K. "Dryden's Heroic Plays: a Study of Their Theory and Practice," IJES, IX (1968), 87-95.

273 Rasco, Kay Frances Dilworth. "Supernaturalism in the He-

roic Play." Doctoral Dissertation: Northwestern University, 1966. 184pp.

274 Righter, Anne. "Heroic Tragedy," *Restoration Theatre*. Edited by John Russell Brown, and Bernard Harris. (Stratford-Upon-Avon Studies, 6.) London: Edward Arnold (Publishers), Ltd., 1965; New York: Capricorn Books, 1967. Pp. 135-57.

Uses Dryden's plays in a study of the Restoration rivalry between comedy and tragedy.

275 Rodney, Caroline. "Dryden's Tragicomedy." Doctoral Dissertation: Cornell University, 1973. 285pp.

Secret Love, *Marriage à la Mode*, *The Spanish Fryar*, and *Love Triumphant*. Rodney finds that "double-plot tragicomedy affords Dryden a chance to express with particular clarity his ideas about the necessity for restraining selfish passion, not expecting perfection in life, submitting to the authority of divinely-appointed monarchs, and awaiting the will of Divine Providence."

276 Tisch, J. H. "Late Baroque Drama--a European Phenomenon?" *Proceeding of the Vth Congress of the International Comparative Literature Association*, Universite de Belgrade. Amsterdam: Swets and Zeitlinger, 1969. Pp. 125-36.

277 Waith, Eugene M. *The Herculean Hero in Marlowe, Shakespeare and Dryden*. London: Chatto & Windus, Ltd.; New York: Columbia University Press, 1962. 224pp.

Examines the relationship of *All for Love* to *The Conquest of Granada* and *Aureng-Zebe*. Reviewed by Bruce King in DS, II, 222-3. Part of chapter six reprinted as "All for Love," in *Restoration Dramatists*, edited by Earl Miner (Englewood Cliffs, 1966), 51-62; Pp. 188-200 reprinted as "The Herculean Hero," in #157 above, 72-82.

278 _____. *Ideas of Greatness: Heroic Drama in England*. London: Routledge & Kegan Paul, Ltd., 1971. Pp. 203-35, 253-65.

279 Winterbottom, John. "The Development of the Hero in Dryden's Tragedies," JEGP, LII (1953), 161-73.

Aureng-Zebe, *The Conquest of Granada*, *The Indian Emperour*, and *Tyrannick Love*. The movement is away from the "hero as social iconoclast toward the hero as embodiment of a social ideal," with Dryden steering "a middle course between Marlowe and Chapman."

280 Youngren, Mary Ann. "The Marks of Sovereignty: Authority

and Force in Dryden's Heroic Dramas." Doctoral Dissertation: Harvard University, 1968.

281 Zebouni, Salma Assir. Dryden: a Study in Heroic Characterization. (Louisiana State University Studies, Humanistic Series, 16.) Baton Rouge: Louisiana State University Press, 1965. vii + 111pp.

"The hero is studied in relation to the plot situation-- that is, the play is considered as drama and not as a rostrum for the voicing of various ideas," she says, and offers "an interpretation of the archetype of the heroic hero."

282 ──────. "The Hero in Dryden's Heroic Tragedy: a Revaluation." Doctoral Dissertation: Louisiana State University, 1963. 224pp.

Relates the heroes to Dryden's milieu and personal development.

On the Operas

283 Crinò, Anna Maria. L'opera letteria di John Dryden. Verona: Fiorini, 1971. 404pp. (Bibliography, 359-92.)

284 Lowens, Irving. "St. Evremond, Dryden, and the Theory of Opera," Criticism, I (1959), 226-48.

285 Zimmerman, Franklin B. Henry Purcell (1659-1695): His Life and Times. London: The Macmillan Company, Ltd.; New York: St. Martin's Press, 1967. xvii + 429pp.

On the Tragedies

286 Anderberg, Gary Timothy. "Idea and Passion: the Development of Dryden's Tragic Drama." Doctoral Dissertation: Stanford University, 1972. 368pp.

Notes a shift "from the intellectual design and adjudicatory function of the heroic plays to the direct appeal of the emotions, especially pity and compassion, which characterizes the later tragedies."

287 Cunningham, John E. "John Dryden," Restoration Drama. London: Evans Brothers, Ltd., 1966. Pp. 59-76.

An essay focusing on rhyme in tragedy.

288 Ebbs, John Dale. The Principle of Poetic Justice Illustrated in Restoration Tragedy. (Salzburg Studies in English Literature, 4.) Salzburg: Universität Salzburg, 1973. 211pp.

Using the standards and theory of the Restoration, Ebbs examines King Arthur, 87-93, The Conquest of Granada, 105-16, All for Love, 131-40, Don Sebastian, 146-52, and Troilus and Cressida, 164-71.

289 Jeune, Simon. "Hamlet d'Otway, Macbeth de Dryden, ou Shakespeare en France en 1714," RLC, XXXVI (1962), 560-4.

290 King, Bruce. "Dryden's Ark: the Influence of Filmer," SEL, VII (1967), 403-14.

One of Dryden's images for the Restoration, Noah's Ark, comes from Filmer's Patriarcha.

291 McCollum, John I., Jr. "Dryden's Dramatic Adaptations: the Tragedies." Doctoral Dissertation: Duke University, 1956.

292 Park, Hugh Winston. "Revenge in Restoration Tragedy." Doctoral Dissertation: University of Utah, 1959. 230pp.

He finds that the Restoration "began with the static and simply designed dramas by D'Avenant in which revenge was little used because of strict codes of honor which rigidly bound the hero. The period ended with static and simply designed drama in which the hero could not act because his code of honor had completely collapsed."

293 Rothstein, Eric. Restoration Tragedy: Form and the Process of Change. Madison and London: University of Wisconsin Press, 1967. xii + 194pp.

Rothstein uses 14 of Dryden's plays in a study showing how the Renaissance didactic moral purpose for tragedy yielded to the Restoration's need for experimentation in drama in an age of empiricism.

294 Simpson, Friench, Jr., "The Relationship Between Character and Action in Neo-Classical Tragedy, with Special Reference to Some Tragedies of John Dryden." Doctoral Dissertation: Stanford University, 1951. 184pp.

295 Stalling, Donald Langhorne. "From Dryden to Lillo: the Course of English Tragedy, 1660-1731." Doctoral Dissertation: The University of Texas at Austin, 1969.

165pp.

296 Winterbottom, John A. "Patterns of Piety: Studies in the Intellectual Background of Dryden's Tragedies." Doctoral Dissertation: Yale University, 1948.

Not in Monk (#77 above) or Keast (#74 above).

297 _____. "The Place of Hobbesian Ideas in Dryden's Tragedies," JEGP, LVII (1958), 665-83.

Makes the following points concerning the plays: "human behavior emerges from an internal struggle in which there is a genuine possibility that virtue may win out"; and, "man is bound to society naturally, not politically." In # 177 above, 374-94.

298 _____. "Stoicism in Dryden's Tragedies," JEGP, LXI (1962), 868-83.

Winterbottom argues that stoicism "restrained the powerful" and gave "resignation to the victims of power."

On Specific Dramas

Albion and Albanius (1685):

299 Muir, Donald Beldon. "John Dryden's Albion and Albanius and King Arthur: an Analysis of Operatic Form." Master's Thesis: Stanford University, 1955.

All for Love; or, The World Well Lost (1677): (see #s 609, 617)

300 Brown, Richard P. "Anthony and Cleopatra and All for Love: a Comparison of Two Dramatic Methods." Master's Thesis: Indiana University, 1960.

301 Caracciolo, Peter. "Dryden and the Antony and Cleopatra of Sir Charles Sedley," ES, L (Supplement, 1969), xliv-l. (Parallels.)

302 Cook, M. G. "The Restoration Ethos of Byron's Classical Plays," PMLA, LXXIX (1964), 569-78.

Essays Dryden's influence on Byron through parallels between Sardanapalus and All for Love.

303 Davies, H. Neville. "Dryden, Hobbes, and the Nimble Span-

iel," N&Q, X (1963), 349-50.

Replies to #509 below indicating Hobbes's Leviathan as the source of Dryden's spaniel imagery.

304 _____. "Dryden's All for Love and Sedley's Antony and Cleopatra," N&Q, XIV (1967), 221-7.

Parallel passages illustrate Dryden's superiority.

305 _____. "All for Love and Sedley's Antony and Cleopatra," N&Q, XV (1968), 65.

306 _____. "Dryden's All for Love and Thomas May's The Tragedie of Cleopatra Queen of Aegypt," N&Q, XII (1965), 139-44.

Act I of Dryden's play is indebted to May's 1626 drama. In #157 above, 112-115.

307 _____. "Shakespeare's Sonnet LXVI Echoed in All for Love," N&Q, XV (1968), 262-3.

Shakespeare's "And simple-Truth, miscalde Simplicitie," becomes Ventidius's "In desparate sloth, miscalled Philosophy."

308 Emerson, Everett H., Harold E. Davis and Ira Johnson. "Intention and Achievement in All for Love," CE, XVII (1955), 84-7.

Examines the apparent contradiction between the preface and the play on the point of passionate "unlawful" love. In #157 above, 55-60

309 Faas, K. E. "Some Notes on Dryden's All for Love," Anglia, LXXXVIII (1970), 341-6.

Relates Dryden's play to Mary Sidney's Antonie, 1590, and Sedley's Antony and Cleopatra, 1677.

310 Ferry, Anne Davidson. Milton and the Miltonic Dryden. Cambridge, Mass.: Harvard University Press; London: Oxford University Press, 1968. 238pp.

Part II examines All for Love's stylistic indebtedness to Milton. Reviewed in RES, XXI, 82-4.

311 Forker, Charles R. "Romeo and Juliet and the 'Cydnus' Speech in Dryden's All for Love," N&Q, IX (1962), 382-3.

On the characterizations of Cleopatra and Juliet, and other similarities between the plays.

312 Freedman, Morris. "All for Love and Samson Agonistes," N&Q, III (1956), 514-17.

Argues that "the verbal, thematic, and critical connections" between the works "indicate that Dryden not only knew Milton well but was modifying Shakespeare through him." Abridged in #157 above, 108-112.

313 Frost, William. "Dryden's Prologue and Epilogue to All for Love," Exp, X (1951), Query #1.

Conjectures that "plenteous autumn' and the "last age" refer to the period of Elizabethan and Jacobean drama, noting a deliberate contrast between prol. lines 33-40 and epil., 20-31.

314 Goggin, L. P. "'This Bow of Ulysses,'" Essays and Studies in Language and Literature. (Duquesne Studies, Philological Series, 5.) Herbert H. Petit, general editor. Pittsburgh: Duquesne University Press, 1964. Pp. 49-86.

Applies the opinions of persons other than Neander in Of Dramatic Poesy, an Essay to Dryden's play, noting sources, historical details, use of reason, the unities, and concluding that Shakespeare wrote a more memorable play but Dryden a more correct one.

315 Hagstrum, Jean H. The Sister Arts: the Tradition of literary Pictorialism and English Poetry from Dryden to Gray. Chicago: University of Chicago Press, 1958. Pp. 173-209.

Pp. 185-97 reprinted as "Ideal Form in All for Love," in #157 above, 61-71.

316 Heise, Howard Sherman. "A Comparative Study of Shakespeare's Antony and Cleopatra and Dryden's All for Love." Master's Thesis" University of South Dakota, 1963.

317 Hennings, Thomas P. "The Glorious and Loving Hero: Intellectual and Dramatic Backgrounds of Dryden's All for Love." Doctoral Dissertation: University of Wisconsin, 1971. 203pp.

Hennings concludes "The moral positions represented" are "brought into a delicate agreement as Dryden leaves to his audience the task of making the final judgement about the glorious lovers."

318 Hughes, Derek W. "The Significance of All for Love," ELH, XXXVII (1970), 540-63.

States that the play is a "portrayal of man's isolation in life within the prison of his imperfect perception." Imagery study.

319 Hughes, R. E. "Dryden's All for Love: the Sensual Dilemma," DC, III (1960), 68-74.

Calls the play "a psychological drama in a very full sense: the account of a powerful compulsion in Antony which is incapable of resolution, for it is self-defeating and self-negating. It is the sensual dilemma of virility wasting itself to prove itself. It is a tragedy of the inability of man to choose, because of the dark forces of negation which lie beyond his reason."

320 Johnson, James W. "John Dryden, his Times, and All for Love," Essays in Honor of Richeborg Gaillard McWilliams. Edited by Howard Creed. Birmingham, Ala.: Birmingham-Southern College, 1970. Pp. 21-8.

Reviewed by M. A. Owings in SAB, XXXVI, 93.

321 Kearful, F. J. "'Tis Past Recovery': Tragic Consciousness in All for Love," MLQ, XXXIV (1973), 227-46.

Explores "a deliberately contrived, affectively induced modification of the audience's consciousness through a cumulative process of psychologically emotive appeals."

322 King, Bruce. "Dryden's Intent in All for Love," CE, XXIV (1963), 267-71.

King states that Dryden did not write the play "for the excellency of the moral" but for dramatic purposes expressed in Heads of an Answer to Rymer's Remarks on the Tragedies of the Last Age, 1677.

323 Klima, S. "Some Unrecorded Borrowings from Shakespeare in Dryden's All for Love," N&Q, X (1963), 415-18.

A dozen parallel passages in Shakespeare; and, the concluding couplet in Dryden suggests a similar situation in Racine's Berenice.

324 Kossman, H. "A Note on Dryden's All for Love," ES, XXXI (1950), 99-100.

Interprets the passage on the human soul, V, 165ff., as "immaterial, incorruptible, and without extension."

325 Nazareth, Peter. "All for Love: Dryden's Hybrid Play," ESA, VI (1963), 154-63.

326 Nelson, Raymond S. "Eros Lost," IEY, XXII (1972), 42-7.

Dryden wastes "potentially explosive moments of passion."

327 Palmer, Roderick. "Treatments of Antony and Cleopatra," CEA, XXVII (1965), 8-9.

328 Reinert, Otto. "Passion and Pity in All for Love: a Reconsideration," The Hidden Sense and Other Essays. Edited by Kristian Schmid. (Norwegian Studies in English, 9.) Oslo: Universitets-verlaget; New York: Humanities Press, Inc., 1963. Pp. 159-95.

Concludes that "passion's final paradoxical triumps over reason takes place in a moment of heroic grandeur, pity ceding to passion, sentiment to magnitude, as the imperial lovers, 'giving laws to half mankind,' extend their romantic dominion to 'late posterity.'" Reprinted in #157 above, 83-98.

329 Rice, Julian C. "The Allegorical Dollabella," CLAJ, XIII (1970), 402-7.

States that "Dolabella's love" and "Antony's rage" comprise the "major actions of Act IV of All for Love."

330 Ringler, Richard N. "Dryden at the House of Busirane," ES, XLIX (1968), 224-9.

I, i, of Dryden's play and The Faerie Queene, III, xii.

331 Schlueter, Anne R. "John Dryden's All for Love, eine Interpretation." Doctoral Dissertation: Georg-August Universität, Gottingen.

332 Starnes, D. T. "Imitation of Shakespeare in Dryden's All for Love," TSLL, VI (1964), 39-46.

Borrowings from As You Like It, Coriolanus, Julius Caesar, Macbeth, The Merchant of Venice, and Othello.

333 Suckling, Norman. "Dryden in Egypt: Reflections on All for Love," DUJ, XLV (1952), 2-7.

Holds that the play is a "spoken opera." Reprinted in #157 above, 46-54.

334 Tritt, C. S. "The Title of All for Love," ELN, X (1973), 273-5.

Interprets "Well Lost" as "decorously lost," noting that Antony and Cleopatra redeem themselves situationally.

335 Weinbrot, Howard D. "Alexas in All for Love: His Geneo-

logy and Function," SP, LXIV (1967), 625-39.

Notes the influences on the characterization from previous plays and argues that Dryden's Alexas is fully developed to function within the play's design of good and evil contrasts.

Amphitryon; or, The Two Socias (1690):

336   Lindberger, Örjan. The Transformations of Amphitryon. (Stockholm Studies in the History of Literature, 1.) Stockholm: Almqvist and Wiksell, 1958. 234pp.

337   Merzbach, Margaret Kober. "The Third Source of Dryden's Amphitryon," Anglia, LXXIII (1955), 213-14.

   Heywood's Silver Age.

338   _____. "Kleist and Dryden," SCB, XXI (1961), 11-16.

   Detailed parallels illustrate Dryden's influence on Kleist's Amphitryon.

The Assignation; or, Love in a Nunnery (1672):

339   Moore, Frank Harper. Heroic Comedy: a New Interpretation of Dryden's Assignation," SP, LI (1954), 585-98.

   Argues that Dryden attempted "to please persons of refinement by mixing high comedy of the sort he had already written, with still higher, heroic comedy."

340   Seward, Patricia M. "Was the English Restoration Theatre Significantly Influenced by the Spanish Drama," RLC, XLVI (1972), 95-125.

   Spanish borrowings in The Assignation.

341   Zamonski, John A. "The Spiritual Nature of Carnal Love in Dryden's Assignation," ETJ, XXV (1973), 189-92.

   The play "develops the idea of love's essential religiosity by exploiting a sacramental motif; that is, Dryden manipulates Holy Orders, Communion, Matrimony, Baptism, Confession, and Confirmation in one episode after another."

Aureng-Zebe (1675): (see #s 394, 420)

342   Alssid, Michael W. "The Design of Dryden's Aureng-Zebe,"
      JEGP, LXIV (1965), 452-69.

      Essays Dryden's mythic structure.

343   Broich, Ulrich. "Libertin und heroischer Held: das Drama
      der englischen Restaurationzeit und seine Leitbilder,"
      Anglia, LXXV (1967), 34-57.

      Discusses heroic characterization in Aureng-Zebe and
      Tyrannick Love.

344   Brooks, Harold F. "Dryden's Aureng-Zebe: Debts to Cor-
      neille and Racine," RLC, XLVI (1972), 5-34.

      Corneille's Nicomede and Rodogune and Racine's Bajazet,
      Mithridate, and Britannicus.

345   Chowdhury, Munir. Drāiḍena o Ḍi. Ela. Rāya. Dacca:
      Dacca University, 1963. 62pp.

      Title in Bengali, transliterated as above. (Dryden and
      D. L. Roy, i.e., Dwijendra Lal Roy.)

346   Dixon, P. "Pope and Dryden," N&Q, XIII (1966), 460-1.

      The Epistle to a Lady, 1735, lines 27-8 may "owe some-
      thing" to Aureng-Zebe, II, 125-7.

347   Kirsch, Arthur C. "The Significance of Dryden's Aureng-
      Zebe," ELH, XXIX (1962), 160-74.

      Argues that sentimental elements found in later plays
      are found in Aureng-Zebe.

348   Le Comte, Edward S. "Samson Agonistes and Aureng-Zebe,"
      EA, XI (1958), 18-22.

349   Martin, Leslie Howard. "Aureng-Zebe and the Ritual of the
      Persian King," MP, LXXI (1973), 169-71.

      States that Dryden's familiarity with "the literary mo-
      tif of a condemned Shah may date back to his Westminster
      school days under Richard Busby."

350   _____. "Consistency of Dryden's Aureng-Zebe," SP,
      LXX (1973), 306-28.

      Sees the play as a restoring of the balance, not a re-
      pudiation, of heroic values.

351 Morton, Richard. "'By no strong passion swayed'; a Note on John Dryden's Aureng-Zebe," ESA, I (1958), 59-68.

352 Newman, Robert S. "Irony and the Problem of Tone in Dryden's Aureng-Zebe," SEL, X (1970), 439-58.

> Calls the play "one whose heroic elements are united with irony and satire to suggest a hopeful yet basically skeptical attitude towards the very possibilities of love and honor," and notes that Aureng-Zebe comes at the end of a period of heroic drama.

Cleomenes, The Spartan Heroe (1692):

353 Archer, Stanley. "A Performance of Dryden's Cleomenes," N&Q, XVIII (1971), 460-1.

> Christmas, 1695, with the prologue by Matthew Prior.

354 Brossman, Sidney W. "A Critical Edition of Dryden's Cleomenes, The Spartan Heroe." Doctoral Dissertation: University of Southern California, 1955. 930pp.

355 ———. "Dryden's Cassandra and Congreve's Zara," N&Q, III (1956), 102-3.

> Calls for more investigation of Dryden's later plays to determine their influences upon later playwrights.

356 ———. "Dryden's Cleomenes and Fletcher's Bonduca," N&Q, IV (1957), 66-8.

> In his borrowings Dryden changed Fletcher's restrained classical language, according to Brossman.

357 Golden, Samuel A. "Dryden's Cleomenes and Theophilus Parsons," N&Q, XIII (1966), 380.

> Notes Dryden's concern for young poets, illustrated by his publishing Parson's poem of praise in the 1693 edition of Cleomenes.

The Conquest of Granada by the Spaniards, two parts (1670-1):

358 Biddle, Evelyn Q. "A Critical Study of the Influence of the Classical and Christian Traditions Upon the Character of the Hero as Revealed Through Concepts of 'Love'

and 'Honor' in Three Restoration Heroic Tragedies."
Doctoral Dissertation: University of Southern California, 1967. 316pp.

Dryden's play, Orrery's Henry V, and Settle's The Empress of Morocco.

359 Compton, Gail Howard. "The Metaphor of Conquest in Dryden's The Conquest of Granada." Doctoral Dissertation: University of Florida, 1968. 133pp.

States that "Conquest becomes a rich metaphor in Dryden's heroic play, one which describes a process that encompasses human flux from the smallest unit of the single individual to the larger unit of the political order."

360 Coshow, Betty Gay. "Dryden's 'Zambra Dance,'" Exp, XVI (1957), #16.

Analyses of meter, tone, and myth. See #361.

361 King, Bruce. "Dryden's 'Zambra Dance,'" Exp, XVIII (1959), #18.

Reply to #360 above. King states that "the theme of fancy underlies the subject of the poem," and ties the song to the play. He says the source of the poem is Hobbes's Leviathan, "Of Imagination," I, 2.

Don Sebastian, King of Portugal (1689):

362 _____. "Don Sebastian: Dryden's Moral Fable," Sew Rev, LXX (1962), 651-70.

Essays the dramatic structure in the context of French neo-classical criticism.

363 Lemly, John William. "Into Winter Quarters Gone: the Last Plays of Jonson and Dryden." Doctoral Dissertation: Yale University, 1972. 259pp.

Finds that Dryden's later plays are more even in "style and characterization" than the heroic dramas, and notes treatments of a mutability theme "with a domestic focus that prizes qualities of compassion and resignation."

364 Moore, John Robert. "Dryden and Rupert Brooke," MLR, LIV (1959), 226.

Notes borrowings from Brooke's sonnet, The Sòldier, in Don Sebastian's first speech.

The Duke of Guise (1682): (See also #941)

365 Bachorik, Lawrence L. "The Duke of Guise and Dryden's Vindication: a New Consideration," ELN, X (1973), 208-12.

Argues that the play refers to 1682 politics and that "Dryden is less than sincere in the Vindication."

366 Hinnant, Charles H. "The Background of the Early Version of Dryden's The Duke of Guise," ELN, VI (1968, 102-6.

A discussion of the Solemn League and Covenant's relationship to the play and Dryden's politics.

367 King, Bruce. "Anti-Whig Satire in The Duke of Guise," ELN, II (1965), 190-3.

Conjectures that whiggism in the play comes from Filmer's Patriarcha, Shadwell's Epistle to the Tories, and the anonymous A Letter from a Person of Quality to His Friend Concerning His Majesties Late Declaration.

368 Verdurmen, John Peter. "Lee, Dryden, and the Restoration Tragedy of Concernment." Doctoral Dissertation: Stanford University, 1973. 320pp.

Finds that Dryden's two collaborations with Lee "were put together according to the principles that underlie Lee's earlier tragedies," and suggests that the older playwright "sensed the way the wind was blowing in English drama and became in time the student of his young, innovative collegue."

An Evening's Love; or, The Mock Astrologer (1668):

369 Allen, Ned B. "The Source's of Dryden's The Mock Astrologer," PQ, XXXVI (1957), 453-64.

Details borrowing's from Molière, Quinault, Corneille, and Madeleine de Scudéry, noting that the Wildblood-Jacintha plot is Dryden's invention.

370 Fiorino, Salvatore. John Dryden: The Mock Astrologer.

Fonti e Pseudo Fonti. Palermo: G. Li Bassi, 1959.

Source study with a bibliography.

371 Griffith, Richard Randolph. "Science and Pseudo-Science in the Imagery of John Dryden." Doctoral Dissertation: The Ohio State University, 1956. 178pp.

Finds Dryden began his study of astrology in 1668 and that it was "in some way connected with the writing of An Evening's Love: or, The Mock Astrologer, but whether as result of cause is not ascertainable." Griffith notes the existence of two horoscopes by Elias Ashmole for "the poet and his eldest son."

372 O'Regan, M. J. "Two Notes on French Reminiscences in Restoration Comedy," Hermathena, XCII (1959), 63-70.

Dryden's play and Congreve's The Way of the World.

The Indian Emperour; or, The Conquest of Mexico by the Spaniards (1665):

373 Alssid, Michael W. "The Perfect Conquest: a Study of Theme, Structure, and Characters in Dryden's The Indian Emperour," SP, LIX (1962), 539-59.

Focusses on Cortez who "emerges not only as an instrument of Destiny but as a private agent driven by strong sexual and military passions learning lessons of suffering and control."

374 Freehafer, John. "Dryden's Indian Emperour," Exp, XXVII (1968), #24.

Virgil's Jason (Georgics) may be a source for the expedition of Cortez.

375 Jackson, Wallace. "Dryden's Emperour and Lillo's Merchant: the Relevant Bases of Action," MLQ, XXVI (1965), 536-44.

Discusses the concept of a social contract.

376 Kinsley, James. "A Dryden Play at Edinburgh," SHR, XXXIII (1954), 129-32.

Sees a reference to an Edinburgh performance in the 1684 prologue.

377 Loftis, John. "El príncipe constante and The Indian Emperour," MLR, XLV (1970), 761-7.

Doubt's Calderón's influence on Dryden's play.

378 ──────. "Exploration and Enlightenment: Dryden's The Indian Emperour and Its Background," PQ, XLV (1966), 71-84.

Primitivism, politics, and religion in the play.

379 MacMillan, Dougald. "The Sources of Dryden's The Indian Emperour," HLQ, XIII (1950), 355-70.

Davenant's Cruelty of the Spaniards in Peru and Samuel Purchas's Pilgrimage.

380 Means, James A. "'Mistake into,'" N&Q, XIII (1966), 461.

Sees an influence in the prologue, 16-17, on Pope's Essay on Criticism, 556-7.

381 Miró, César. "México y Perú en la Tragedia clásica occidental," CCLC, C (1965), 66-70.

382 Perkins, Merle E. "Dryden's The Indian Emperour and Voltaire's Alzire," CL, IX (1957), 229-37.

Examines philosophical meaning, historical orientation, and structure in the two plays

383 Ringler, Richard N. "Two Sources for Dryden's The Indian Emperour," PQ, XLII (1963), 423-9.

The Faerie Queene and Donne's First Anniversarie.

384 Shergold, N. D., and Peter Ure. "Dryden and Calderón: a New Spanish Source for The Indian Emperour," MLR, LXI (1966), 369-83.

El Principe Constante.

385 Spector, Robert Donald. "A Dryden Echo in Tennyson," N&Q, CXCVII (1952), 520.

The song from Dryden's play, I, ii, and Lotus Eaters, 13ff, "Why are we weighed."

386 Wilson, John H. "The Duchess of Portsmouth's Players," N&Q, X (1963), 106-7.

The Indian Emperour was produced by an amateur group

before Sept. 30, 1675, but not by the 'Players,' whose existence Wilson doubts.

The Indian Queen (1664): (see #392 below)

387 Arnold, Denis. "Purcell's Indian Queen," Listener, LXXXIX (1973), 285.

388 Smith, John H. "The Dryden-Howard Collaboration," SP, LI (1954), 54-74.

   Assigns I; II, i: and III of the play to Dryden and suggests that he may have written part of Howard's The Vestal Virgin.

The Kind Keeper; or, Mr. Limberham (1678):

389 Baker, Van R. "Heroic Posturing Satirized: Dryden's Mr. Limberham," PLL, VIII (1972), 370-9.

   Discusses Woodall's martial metaphors.

King Arthur; or, The British Worthy (1691):

390 Gottesman, Lillian. "The Arthurian Romance in English Opera and Pantomime," RECTR, VIII (Nov., 1969), 47-53.

   Dryden's knowledge of the legend.

391 Hitchman, Percy J. "King Arthur at Nottingham: a Notable Revival," TN, XI (1957), 121-8.

   Production notes and diagram for a performance at the University of Nottingham in 1956.

392 Moore, Robert Etheridge. Henry Purcell and the Restoration Theatre. Cambridge, Mass.: Harvard University Press, 1961. Pp. 70-99.

   Discography, 215. The Indian Queen, 155-77, and the Shadwell-Tempest, 178-203.

393 Westrup, J. A. Purcell. (The Master Musicians Series.) London: J. M. Dent & Sons, Ltd.; New York: Farrar,

Straus and Giroux, Inc., 1965. Pp. 71-3.

Suggests that Purcell may have criticized Dryden's text.

Marriage A-la-Mode (1672): (see #411)

394 Geist, Edward Valentine, Jr. "Temple, Dryden, and Saint-Evremond: a Study in Libertine Aesthetics and Moral Values." Doctoral Dissertation: University of Virginia, 1971. 223pp.

Examines the types of love in the play.

395 Heath-Stubbs, John. The Pastoral. London: Oxford University Press, 1969. Pp. 47-8.

Analyzes II, i, 454ff. (Palmyra. "Do you remember, when their tasks were done," etc.)

396 King, Bruce. "Dryden's Marriage à la Mode," DS, IV (1965), 28-37.

Dryden's design includes "an extended comparison between fashionable Restoration society and Thomas Hobbes' theory that man in his natural state is permanently at war to conquer the property of others."

397 Okerlund, Arlene Naylor. "Literature and its Audience: the Reader in Action in Selected Works of Spenser, Dryden, Thackeray, and T. S. Eliot." Doctoral Dissertation: University of California at San Diego, 1969. 234pp.

Her reader-response approach to Marriage à la Mode finds that "Restoration man" was a "self-regarding creature to whom questions of honor, virtue, duty and love" were "mere exasperations in his efforts to gratify sexual desire."

398 Reichert, John. "A Note on Buckingham and Dryden," N&Q, IX (1962), 220.

The basis for The Rehearsal's satire of Dryden's play, according to Reichert, is its use of letters.

The Mistaken Husband (1675):

399 Wilson, John H. "Six Restoration Play Dates," N&Q, IX

(1962), 221-3.

Production dates for this play and Oedipus.

Oedipus (1678):

400 Kallich, Martin. "Oedipus: from Man to Archetype," CLS, III (1966), 33-46.

Notes the sentimental element in the Dryden-Lee play.

401 Maxwell, J. C. "Dryden's Epilogue to Oedipus, 5-6," N&Q, IX (1962), 384-5.

Was influenced by Horace's Ars Poetica, 38-40.

The Rival Ladies (1664):

402 Biggins, D. "Source Notes for Dryden, Wycherley, and Otway," N&Q, III (1956), 298-301.

Secret Love; or, The Maiden-Queen (1667):

403 Gagen, Jean E. The New Woman: Her Emergence in English Drama, 1600-1730. New York: Twayne Publishers, Inc., 1954. Pp. 142-3, 147-9.

404 Hume, Robert D. "Dryden, James Howard, and the Date of All Mistaken," PQ, LI (1972), 422-9.

Argues that the play's date is 1665 and is, therefore, not an imitation of Secret Love.

405 Martin, Leslie Howard. "Dryden and the Art of Transversion," CD, VI (1972), 3-13.

Discusses Dryden's borrowings from Le Grand Cyrus, noting that he changed its ending "to point up the triumph of love and virtue."

406 Sutherland, James R. "The Date of James Howard's All Mistaken, or, the Mad Couple," N&Q, XI (1964), 339-40.

Conjecture's that Dryden's play was derived from it.

The Secular Masque (1700):

407   Dearing, Bruce. "Some Views of a Beast," MLN, LXXI
      (1956), 326-9.

      Finds "Thy chase had a beast in view," line 87, to be
      "elusive."

408   Roper, Alan. "Dryden's Secular Masque," MLQ, XXIII
      (1962), 29-40.

      Dryden's historical point of view in the masque may be
      derived from Horace's Carmen Secularae.

Sir Martin Mar-all; or, The Feign'd Innocence (1667):

409   Moore, F. H. "The Composition of Sir Martin Mar-all,"
      SP (Extra Series, Jan., 1967), 27-38.

      Analyzes the comedy, essaying its history, sources,
      and significance to the Dryden canon.

The Spanish Fryar; or, The Double Discovery (1680):

410   Gibb, Carson. "Figurative Structure in Restoration Comedy." Doctoral Dissertation: University of Pennsylvania, 1962. 342pp.

      Finds a unity in seemingly "unrelated" actions in the
      play.

411   Kronenberger, Louis. The Thread of Laughter. New York:
      Alfred A. Knopf, 1952. Pp. 81-8.

      Discusses the comic plots in this play and Marriage à
      la Mode, 88-91.

The State of Innocence, And Fall of Man (1673):

412   Evans, G. Blakemore. "Edward Ecclestone: His Relationship to Dryden and Milton," MLR, XLIV (1949), 550-2.

      Discusses The State of Innocence and Paradise Lost

and Dryden's influence upon Ecclestone's Noah's Flood.

413 Freedman, Morris. "Dryden's 'Memorable Visit' to Milton," HLQ, XVIII (1955), 99-108.

Holds that Dryden's motive for the visit was to determine "how the same matter" compared in rhyme and blank verse.

414 _____. "The 'Tagging' of Paradise Lost: Rhyme in Dryden's The State of Innocence," MQ, V (1971), 18-22.

Conjectures that the play began as a rhymed epic and turned into a verse drama, which may have accounted for its production failure.

415 Hamilton, Marion H. "Dryden's The State of Innocence: an Old-Spelling Edition with a Critical Study of the Early Printed Texts and Manuscripts." Doctoral Dissertation: University of Virginia, 1952. 231pp.

416 Harris, Bernard. "'That Soft Seducer, Love': Dryden's The State of Innocence and Fall of Man," Approaches to Paradise Lost: York Tercentenary Lectures. Edited by C. A. Patrides. London: Edward Arnold (Publishers), Ltd.; Toronto: University of Toronto Press, 1968. Pp. 120-136.

An essay on Dryden's dramatic intention.

417 King, Bruce. "The Significance of Dryden's State of Innocence," SEL, IV (1964), 371-91.

Examines the theme of "moral disobedience which results from the nature of man's appetite, pride, and unrest."

418 Kolb, Gwin J. "Johnson Echoes Dryden," MLN, LXXIV (1959), 212-13.

Parallels between two lines of The State of Innocence and The Vanity of Human Wishes.

419 Legouis, Pierre. "Dryden plus Miltonien que Milton?" EA, XX (1967), 370-7.

Paradise Lost and Dryden's dramatic version.

420 McFadden, George. "Dryden's 'Most Barren Period'--and Milton," HLQ, XXIV (1961), 283-96.

Argues that Dryden was "developing a technique of internal reinforcement of sound, in the manner of Vergil and Milton," in The State of Innocence and Aureng-Zebe.

421 Stock, Reed Clark. "Milton in Musical and Theatrical Adaptation." Doctoral Dissertation: Rutgers, The State University, 1968. 153pp.

   Contains a chapter on Dryden and The State of Innocence.

422 Williamson, George. "Dryden's View of Milton," Milton and Others. Chicago and London: University of Chicago Press, 1965. Pp. 103-21.

   Essays Dryden's admiration for Milton.

The Tempest; or, The Enchanted Island (1667):

423 Aycock, Wendell Marshall. "The Irrepressible Characters of Shakespeare's The Tempest: Sequels and Re-creations." Doctoral Dissertation: University of South Carolina, 1969. 195pp.

   Discusses the "distinctive effects" derived "by an alternate dependence upon and departure from the events" of Shakespeare's play.

424 Casanave, Don Sheldon. "Shakespeare's The Tempest in a Restoration Context: a Study of Dryden's The Enchanted Island." Doctoral Dissertation: The University of Michigan, 1972. 214pp.

   Casanave finds that Dryden "develops five themes already in Shakespeare's work--primitivism, magic, religion, politics, and love--according to the thought of his period and his own personal beliefs."

425 Loofbourow, John W. "Robinson Crusoe's Island and the Restoration Tempest," EE, II (1971), 201-7.

   Discusses Defoe and the Restoration versions of The Tempest, especially that of 1674.

426 Mellers, Wilfrid. Harmonious Meeting: a Study of the Relationship between English Music, Poetry, and Theatre, c. 1600-1900. London: Dennis Dobson, n.d. Pp. 220-4.

427 Spencer, Christopher. Five Restoration Adaptations of Shakespeare. Urbana: University of Illinois Press, 1965. Pp. 16-22. (Text, 111-99.)

Troilus and Cressida; or, Truth Found Too Late (1679):

428 Atkins, G. Douglas. "The Function and Significance of the Priest in Dryden's Troilus and Cressida," TSLL, XIII (1971), 29-37.

   Examines Cahchas's dissembling.

429 Bernhardt, William. "Shakespeare's Troilus and Cressida and Dryden's Truth Found Too Late," SQ, XX (1969), 129-41.

   Finds that Dryden's "revision directs our attention to the play's real center--Troilus."

430 Boatner, Janet Williams. "Criseyde's Character in the Major Writers from Benoit through Dryden: the Changes and Their Significance." Doctoral Dissertation: The University of Wisconsin, 1970. 254pp.

   Concludes that Dryden's play "is the reflection of a world of fragmented values--not the deliberate portrayal of fragmentation, which might have resulted in a very good play--but the deluded presentation of philosophical and artistic fragmentation as Truth and Beauty."

431 Lavine, Anne Rabiner. "'This Bow of Ulysses': Shakespeare's Troilus and Cressida and Its Imitation by Dryden." Doctoral Dissertation: Bryn Mawr College, 1961. 415pp.

   Examines Dryden's theory and practice and notes that his real achievement is stylistic.

432 Maurer, Wallace. "From Renaissance to Neo-Classic," N&Q, V (1958), 287.

   Examines Ulysses speech on degree in Shakespeare's play and Dryden's consolidated version.

433 Muir, Kenneth. "Three Shakespeare Adaptations," PLPLSLHS, VIII (1959), 233-40.

434 Newell, Rosalie. "Troilus and Cressida, or, Truth Found Too Late: a Study of External and Internal Form in Dryden's Critical Theory and Dramatic Practice." Doctoral Dissertation: University of California at Los Angeles, 1972. 336pp.

   Illustrates Dryden's belief "that the reconciliation of unity with inclusiveness makes it possible to create a 'perfect image' of life which is a 'perfect work' of art as well--to suggest the complexity of the world and yet create the special pleasure and intense instructiveness of art."

435 Nichols, James W. "Shakespeare as a Character in Drama: 1679-1899," ETJ, XV (1963), 24-32.

The prologue to Troilus and Cressida, 1679.

436 Smith, Denzell S. "Dryden's Purpose in Adapting Shakespeare's Troilus and Cressida," BSUF, X (1969), 49-52.

How Shakespeare's deracinated universe was altered "to exhibit the presence of order."

Tyrannick Love; or, The Royal Martyr (1669) (see #343 above):

437 Adams, Henry Hitch. "A Prompt Copy of Dryden's Tyrannick Love," SB, IV (1951-2), 170-4.

Discoveries concerning "theatrical practice" and "production methods" at the King's Company.

438 Jaquith, William George. "Dryden's Tyrannick Love and All for Love." Doctoral Dissertation: University of California at Los Angeles, 1973. 444pp.

He argues that Tyrannick Love, "certainly heroic, is not really tragic either in tone or structure. And All for Love, certainly tragic in tone and structure, is only superficially heroic."

439 King, Bruce. "Dryden, Tillotson, and Tyrannick Love," RES, XVI (1965), 364-77.

Argues for "parallels between St. Catherine's speeches and Tillotson's early sermons," noting that she articulates Dryden's "Latitudinarian Anglican" views.

440 Novak, Maximillian E. "The Demonology of Dryden's Tyrannick Love and 'Anti-Scott,'" ELN, IV (1966), 95-8.

Finds the source of Nakar and Damilcar in "A Discourse Concerning the Nature and Substance of Devils and Spirits," in Discovery of Witchcraft, 1665, by Reginald Scot.

The Wild Gallant (1663):

441 Cecil, C. D. "Delicate and Indelicate Puns in Restoration Comedy," MLR, LXI (1966), 572-8.

On Dryden's attitude toward punning.

442 Cooke, Arthur L. "Two Parallels between Dryden's Wild Gallant and Congreve's Love for Love," N&Q, I (1954), 27-8.

Discusses getting married in the dark and talking someone into illness.

443 Moore, Frank H. "Dr. Pelling, Dr. Pell, and Dryden's Lord Nonsuch," MLR, XLIX (1954), 349-51

Dryden's characterization was based on Dr. Pell.

444 Osenberg, F. C. "The Prologue to Dryden's Wild Gallant Re-examined," ELN, VII (1969), 35-9.

On the astrology of the first prologue.

V PROSE:

General Studies

445 Anala, Philip Z. "John Dryden's Place in the Development of Seventeenth-Century English Prose." Doctoral Dissertation: St. Louis University, 1971. 95pp.

446 Sutherland, James R., and Ian Watt. Restoration and Augustan Prose Papers Delivered . . . at the Third Clark Library Seminar, 14 July 1956. Los Angeles: William Andrews Clark Memorial Library, University of California, 1956. 46pp.

447 Wilson, F. P. Seventeenth Century Prose. Five Lectures. Berkeley and Los Angeles: University of California Press, 1960. Pp. 7-11.

Discusses Dryden's language.

On the Dedications

448 Foss, Michael. The Age of Patronage: the Arts in Eng-

land, 1660-1750. Ithaca: Cornell University Press, 1971. Pp. 24-7, 83-5, 103-9.

449   Illo, John. "Dryden, Sylvester, and the Correspondence of Melancholy Winter and Cold Age," ELN, I (1963), 101-4.

Discusses Dryden's condemnation of Sylvester's use of metaphor.

450   Miner, Earl. "Dryden and 'The Magnified Piece of Duncomb,'" HLQ, XXVIII (1964), 93-8..

Dryden's phrase from the epistle in The Hind and the Panther refers to the publisher of Rodriguez's A Treatise of Humilitie, Eleazer Duncan.

451   Sorelius, Gunnar. "The Unities Again: Dr. Johnson and Delusion," N&Q, IX (1962), 466-7.

Dryden's epistle in Love Triumphant ("I have followed the example of Corneille") may have influenced Johnson's Preface to Shakespeare ("It is false that any representation" etc.).

452   Spencer, Terence. "A Byron Plagiarism from Dryden," N&Q, CXCVI (1951), 164.

Notes that Marino Faliero, I, ii, 280-6, is indebted to the epistle in The Rival Ladies ("this worthless present was designed . . . and then either chosen or rejected by the judgement").

453   Sweney, John R. "The Dedication of Thomas Southerne's The Wives Excuse, 1692," Library, XXV (1970), 154-5.

Discusses the printing of Dryden's poem.

454   Waith, Eugene M. "The Voice of Mr. Bayes," SEL, III (1963), 335-43.

Examines the strategy of creating audiences for the heroic plays.

A Defence of the Papers written by the Late King of Blessed Memory and Duchess of York Against the Answer made to them (1686):

455   Miner, Earl. "Dryden as Prose Controversialist: His Role in 'A Defence of Royal Papers,'" PQ, XLIII (1964),

412-19.

Disputes Charles E. Ward's argument that Dryden wrote only the defence of the Duchess' paper. (See #120 above, p. 219.)

On the Letters
(See #963)

456 Adams, Henry H. "A Note on the Date of a Dryden Letter," MLN, LXIV (1949), 528-31.

Dates the letter to William Walsh, July 20, 1693. This letter is #25 in Ward's edition, see #459 below.

457 Barnard, John. "The Dates of Six Dryden Letters," PQ, XLII (1963), 396-403.

In an answer to #458 below, Barnard upholds Ward's dates for a series of six letters concerning Dryden's progress on the Virgil.

458 Boddy, Margaret P. "Dryden-Lauderdale Relationships, Some Biographical Notes and a Suggestion," PQ, XLII (1963), 267-72.

Holds that a series of six letters by Dryden concerning his Virgil should be dated a year earlier than established, and notes that Lauderdale's Virgil may have been influenced by Dryden's. (See also #955.)

459 Howarth, R. G. "Dryden's Letters," ESA, I (1958), 184-94.

A review of Charles E. Ward's The Letters of John Dryden with Letters Addressed to Him (Durham, 1942; New York, 1965) and a discussion of the subject of Dryden's letters.

460 Legouis, Pierre. "Dryden's Letter to Ormond," MLN, LXVI (1951), 88-92.

Relates the 1698 letter and the verse dedication of "Palamon and Arcite," in Fables Ancient and Modern.

461 Logan, Terence P. "John Dennis's Select Works, 1718, 1721," PBSA, LXV (1971), 155-6.

Calls this edition "clearly the definitive text" and notes that letters to Dryden are included.

On the Literary Criticism and Theory:

comprehensive and miscellaneous studies

462   Aden, John M. "Dryden and Boileau: the Question of Critical Influence," SP, L (1953), 491-509.

   Discusses the translation of Art Poetique and Dryden's general use of Longinus and Boileau.

463   _____. "Dryden and the Imagination: the First Phase," PMLA, LXXIV (1959), 28-40.

   Deals with the terms 'fancy,' 'imagination,' 'humour,' 'wit,' and 'invention' up to 1672.

464   _____. "The Question of Influence in Dryden's Use of the Major French Critics." Doctoral Dissertation: The University of North Carolina at Chapel Hill, 1951. 238pp.

465   _____. "'Nisi Artifex': Dryden and the Poet as Critic," SAB, XXXV (1970), 3-10.

   Notes that for Dryden "sound criticism is as much a matter of character as it is of genius," and compares his statements on the subject with Pope's.

466   Benson, Donald R. "The Artistic Image and Dryden's Conception of Reason," SEL, II (1971), 427-35.

   Finds that the poet assumed the dependability "of the artistic image, never expressing skepticism about it or about the intuitive apprehension it depends on."

467   Bjork, Lennart A. "The 'Inconsistencies' of Dryden's Criticism of Shakespeare," Anglia, XCI (1973), 219-40.

   Emphasizes the practical and argumentative nature of the essays and prefaces, which do not necessarily state abiding beliefs.

468   Blair, Joel. "Dryden on the Writing of Fanciful Poetry," Criticism, XII (1970), 89-104.

   Notes Dryden's traits of scepticism and eclecticism, and of "persistently asking basic questions and seeking permanent principles."

469   Bowers, R. H. "Dryden's Influence on Cuthbert Constable," N&Q, IV (1957), 13-14.

Discusses Dryden's statements on language and a manuscript English dictionary by Constable in the Folger Library.

470 Doederlein, Sue W. "A Compendium of Wit: the Psychological Vocabulary of John Dryden's Literary Criticism." Doctoral Dissertation: Northwestern University, 1970. 167pp.

Finds that Dryden "develops a theory of response that requires a variety of feelings and intensities so that the mind can have its fullest stirrings and then be granted repose."

471 Falle, George Gray. "Dryden: Professional Man of Letters," UTQ, XXVI (1956), 443-55.

Essays Dryden's criticism in the context of Locke's condemnation of poetry.

472 Freedman, Morris. "Milton and Dryden on Tragedy," English Writers of the Eighteenth Century. Edited by John H. Middendorf. New York: Columbia University Press, 1971. Pp. 158-71.

Argues that "While Dryden in his criticism was often tentative, exploratory, hypothesizing, wide-ranging, prolific, occasionally apologetic, Milton was certain, definitive, traditional, peremptory, unqualified, sharply committed, almost cursory, certainly brief."

473 Freehafer, John. "Shakespeare, the Ancients, and Hales of Eton," SQ, XXIII (1972), 63-8.

Dryden on the Shakespearean criticism of John Hales, 1584-1656.

474 Gallagher, Mary Thale. "John Dryden's Use of the Classics in his Literary Criticism." Doctoral Dissertation: Northwestern University, 1960. 245pp.

475 Grace, Joan Carroll. "Tragic Theory in the Critical Works of Thomas Rymer, John Dennis, and John Dryden." Doctoral Dissertation: Columbia University, 1969. 179pp.

Illustrates how their use of Aristotle "was affected by a mixture of Horatian and traditional rhetorical elements introduced by sixteenth-century Italian commentators and codified into a system of general principles and specific rules by French seventeenth-century critics."

476 Hume, Robert David. "Dryden's Criticism." Doctoral Dis-

sertation: University of Pennsylvania, 1969. 270pp.

Aims "to consider the nature of Dryden's critical endeavor, to place his work in context, and to assess the stability of his critical premises."

477 _____. Dryden's Criticism. Ithaca and London: Cornell University Press, 1970. xvii + 236pp.

Examines Dryden's aims, methods, and literary principles in the context of his contemporaries in criticism. Reviewed by P. K. Elkin in AUMLA, XXXVI, 210-16; by Earl Miner in MLQ, XXXII, 439-40; in TLS, Oct. 29, 1971, 1361; by F. L. Huntley in MP, LXXI, 89-90; and, by P. Morgan in ES, LIV, 393-5.

478 Jenkins, Ralph Eugene. "Some Sources of Samuel Johnson's Literary Criticism." Doctoral Dissertation: The University of Texas at Austin, 1969. 186pp.

Illustrates Dryden's influences on Johnson.

479 Jensen, Harvey James. "A Glossary of John Dryden's Critical Terms." Doctoral Dissertation: Cornell University, 1966. 262pp.

Using Watson's text (see #25 above) and The Works of John Dryden, edited by Sir Walter Scott, revised by George Saintsbury (Edinburgh, 1882), Jensen's alphabetized glosses function as a concordance to the critical terms of Dryden and a key to English neo-classical criticism.

480 _____. A Glossary of John Dryden's Critical Terms. Minneapolis: University of Minnesota Press; London: Oxford University Press, 1969. 135pp.

Bibliography, 133-5. Reviewed by William Frost in JEGP, LXXX, 310-12; and by W. F. Myers in YES, I, 259-61.

481 Korshin, Paul J. From Concord to Dissent: Major Themes in English Poetic Theory, 1640-1700. Menston: The Scolar Press, 1973. 264pp.

History of ideas study which examines the light cast on contemporary concepts of art in the theories of Dryden Cleveland, Cowley, Denham, Marvell, Oldham, and Waller.

482 Krupp, Kathleen McCoy. "John Dryden on the Functions of Drama." Doctoral Dissertation: The Florida State University, 1966. 126pp.

Illustrates adherence to Horatian theory and affective

concerns in the essays.

483 Leschetsko, Helen. John Dryden's Dramatic Criticism."
Master's Thesis: Columbia University, 1953.

484 McAleer, John J. "John Dryden: Father of Shakespearean Criticism," SN, XIX (1969), 3.

Summarizes the comments on Shakespeare.

485 Marks, Emerson R. "Pragmatic Poetics: Dryden to Valéry," BR, X (1962), 213-23.

Explores the thesis, "poets who have written criticism have done so primarily to prepare the public for the favorable reception of their own poetry."

486 Marsh, Robert Harrison. "Major Conceptions of Criticism and Taste in England from Dryden to Hume." Doctoral Dissertation: The Johns Hopkins University, 1956.

487 Maurocordato, Alexandre. La Critique en classique Angleterre de la Restauration à la Mort de Joseph Addison; essai de definition. Paris: Didier, 1964. 736pp. (Bibliography, 619-731.)

488 _____. "Positions de la Critique Dramatique chez Dryden," Collection Études Anglaises. Paris: Didier, 1969. Pp. 103-12.

489 Monk, Samuel Holt. "Dryden and the Beginnings of Shakespeare Criticism in the Augustan Age," The Persistence of Shakespeare Idolatry: Essays in Honor of Robert W. Babcock. Edited by Herbert M. Schueller. Detroit: Wayne State University Press, 1964. Pp. 47-75.

Argues that "Dryden's generous praise of Shakespeare and his honest confronting of what seemed the faults of the father of the English stage set the pattern of Shakespeare criticism for subsequent generations."

490 Nänny, Max. John Drydens rhetorische Poetik; Versuch eines Aufbaus aus seinem kritischen Schaffen. (Schweitzer anglistische Arbeiten, 49.) Bern: Franke, 1959. xvii + 101pp.

Reviewed by James Kinsley in RES, XI, 453; by Rudolf Germer in Archiv, CXCVIII, 56; and, by Arvid Løsnes in ES, XLIX, 167-8.

491 Nathanson, Leonard. "The Context of Dryden's Criticism of Donne's and Cowley's Love Poetry," N&Q, IV (1957), 56-9.

Dryden held that "decorum and fidelity to natural purpose are to be observed absolutely, and with a strictness not demanded from other kinds of verse," Nathanson argues.

492 _____. "Dryden, Donne, and Cowley," N&Q, IV (1957), 197-8.

Finds that Dryden's and Waller's criticism of Donne and Cowley "for troubling their mistresses with their learning," has a source in Rapin's Reflections sur la Poetique, 1674, chapter 30.

493 Pechter, Edward Lewis. "John Dryden's Theory of Literature." Doctoral Dissertation: University of California at Berkeley, 1968. 334pp.

Notes that "Dryden conceived of the imagination as a heightening faculty always distinct from the rational and observing faculty of the judgement. Though both are necessary, they are never synthesized."

494 Ramsey, Paul, Jr. "The Image of Nature in John Dryden." Doctoral Dissertation: The University of Minnesota, 1956. 494pp.

Demonstrates four conclusions: "(1) that Dryden's idea of nature provides for a true, flexible, and firmly founded criticism; (2) that Dryden's major achievement in technique is his versification; (3) that Dryden as man, critic, and poet, is more deeply Christian than has been commonly believed; (4) that Dryden's criticism and poetry manifest a sane and exalted view of the world."

495 Romagosa, Sister Edward, O. Carm. "A Compendium of the Opinions of John Dryden." Doctoral Dissertation: Tulane University, 1957. 761pp.

Concludes that "On some major topics in literary matters he was consistently of the same opinion throughout his long life," and notes that "His opinions on individual persons are remarkably consistent."

496 Russell, Doris A. "Dryden's Relations with his Critics." Doctoral Dissertation: Columbia University, 1950. 244pp.

Finds in the prefaces, prologues, epilogues, and epistles "a sensitivity to criticism, springing from a need for approval, which did much to shape the course of Dryden's career."

497 Sellers, William Howard. "Literary Controversies among

Restoration Dramatists, 1660-1685." Doctoral Dissertation: The Ohio State University, 1959.

The Dryden-Howard controversy concerning rhyme in verse drama, noting Dryden's growing awareness of the uses of blank verse.

498 Sellin, Paul R. "The Poetic Theory of Daniel Heinsius and English Criticism of the Seventeenth Century." Doctoral Dissertation: University of Chicago, 1963.

499 Sherwood, John C. "Dryden and the Critical Theories of Tasso," CL, XVIII (1966), 351-9.

Discusses Tasso's influence on Dryden's heroic plays.

500 _____. "Precept and Practice in Dryden's Criticism," JEGP, LXVIII (1969), 432-40.

Argues that Dryden used neo-classical principles in his praise of romantic elements.

501 Sorelius, Gunnar. "The Great Race before the Flood": Pre-Restoration Drama on the Stage and in the Criticism of the Restoration. (Studia Anglistica Uppsaliensa, 4.) Uppsala: Almqvist & Wiksell, 1966. 277pp.

Parts two and three discuss Dryden's theories of tragedy and comedy.

502 Thale, Mary. "Dryden's Critical Vocabulary: the Imitation of Nature," PLL, II (1966), 315-26.

Argues that Dryden's conception of imitating nature was his key to reconciling opposites such as the ancient and the modern, the foreign and the domestic.

503 Watson, George. The Literary Critics: a Study of English Descriptive Criticism. (Pelican Books.) Harmondsworth and Baltimore: Penguin Books, Inc., 1962. 249pp.

504 Weinmann, R. "Shakespeare's Publikum und Platformbühne im Spiegel klassizistischer Kritik. (bei Rymer, Dryden, u.a.)," Bulletin de la Faculte des lettres de Strasbourg, XLIII (1965), 891-1007.

on specific essays

"An Account of the Ensuing Poem, in a Letter to The Honourable Sir Robert Howard," prefixed to Annus Mirabilis (1667):

505 Forrest, James E. "Dryden, Hobbes, Thomas Goodwin, and the Nimble Spaniel," N&Q, IX (1962), 381-2.

   Notes that the spaniel metaphor for wit appears in Goodwin's Vanitie of Thoughts Discovered, 1650.

506 Höltgen, Karl J. "John Dryden's 'nimble spaniel': zur Schnelligkeit der 'inventio' und 'imaginatio,'" Lebende Antik: Symposium für Rudolf Sühnel. Edited by Horst Meller and Hans-Joachim Zimmerman. Berlin: E. Schmidt, 1967. Pp. 233-49.

   Drawing upon classical sources, Höltgen distinguishes between a disciplined and undisciplined type of spaniel corresponding to the imagination as an intellectual faculty that may harmonize with reason or be hostile to it.

507 Kane, Mary Franzita. "John Dryden's Doctrine of Wit as Propriety: a Study of the Terms and Relations involved in the definition of 1677." Doctoral Dissertation: University of Notre Dame, 1958. 418pp.

   Argues that "the basic problems of poet, poetic process, and poem" must be reinterpreted "in the light of his conjunction of a term resonant of the crucial issues of the seventeenth century and a term representing the cardinal principle of classical theory . . . 'fitness.'"

508 Selden, R. "Hobbes, Dryden, and the Ranging Spaniel," N&Q, XX (1973), 388-90.

   Notes the distinctions in the employment of the metaphor, indicating a range of literary, philosophical, and ideological meanings.

509 Watson, George. "Dryden, Hobbes, and the Nimble Spaniel," N&Q, X (1963), 230-1.

   States that the spaniel metaphor is not specifically Puritan, and notes that Dryden first used it in the preface to The Rival Ladies, 1664, and that he employs it in Fables Ancient and Modern as a tribute to Chaucer. (See #303 above.)

"The Author's Apology for Heroic Poetry and Poetic Licence," prefixed to The State of Innocence (1677):

510 Elkin, P. K. "In Defence of Hippocentuars," AUMLA, V (1965), 18-25.

Calls Dryden's defence of the creatures "an example of Augustan uncertainty regarding the limits of verisimilitude in poetry, particularly heroic poetry.

"A Discourse Concerning the Original and Progress of Satire," prefixed to The Satires of Decimus Junius Juvenalis, . . . with the Satires of Aulus Persius Flaccus (1693): (See #s 895, and 932 below)

511 _____. The Augustan Defence of Satire. Oxford: The Clarendon Press; New York: Oxford University Press, 1973. Pp. 146-66.

Examines Dryden's theory and practice in the context of "Smiling versus Savage satire."

512 Elliott, Robert C. The Power of Satire: Magic, Ritual, Art. Princeton: Princeton University Press, 1960. Pp. 116-18.

Extracts the dominant ideas in Dryden's lengthy essay.

513 Frost, William. "Dryden and Satire," SEL, XI (1971), 401-16.

Examines the nature of the term 'satire' as Dryden uses it, noting that he considered it a non-dramatic verse genre.

514 _____. "Dryden's Theory and Practice of Satire," in #156 above, pp. 189-205.

Comments on "Dryden's view of satire in relation to society and his view of satire as a thing in itself."

515 _____. "More about Dryden as Classicist," N&Q, XIX (1972), 23-6.

On his classical scholarship in A Discourse.

516 Hayman, John. "Raillery in Restoration Satire," HLQ, XXXI (1968), 107-22.

Argues that the device of raillery provided a context for social values and satiric commentary. Considers *Of Dramatic Poesy, an Essay*.

517 Kernan, Alvin. *The Plot of Satire*. New Haven: Yale University Press, 1965. Pp. 6-9.

Illustrates Dryden's blending of art and morality.

518 Rudd, Niall. "Dryden on Horace and Juvenal," UTQ, XXXII (1963), 155-69.

Holds that Dryden is "wrong or misleading on almost every major point" in his comparison of these ancients.

Heads of an Answer to Rymer's Remarks on the Tragedies of the Last Age (1677): (See also #564 below)

519 Eade, J. C. "Johnson and Dryden's *Answer to Rymer*," N&Q, XVII (1970), 302.

Disputes Watson's remark, "Johnson clearly had no notion in 1779 that *The Heads* had even been published before." (see #521.)

520 Hume, Robert D. "Dryden's Heads of an Answer to Rymer: Notes toward a Hypothetical Revolution," RES, XIX (1968), 373-86.

Argues that Dryden supports Rymer's premises, and notes, "The supposedly revolutionary side of the *Heads* is not a statement of serious conviction; it is an analysis of forensic possibilities."

521 Watson, George. "Dryden's First Answer to Rymer," SEL, XIV (1963), 17-23.

Calls Dryden's essay "the one critical document in English between the Restoration and Johnson's *Shakespeare* in which the *Poetics* of Aristotle are attacked frontally and without qualification." (And see #519 above.)

Notes and Observations on The Empress of Morocco (1674):

522 Doyle, Anne. "Dryden's Authorship of *Notes and Observations on The Empress of Morocco* (1674)," SEL, VI (1966),

421-45.

Assigns a substantial portion of the essay to Dryden, noting that ideas in the attack appear later in Mac-Flecknoe. (See also #869 below.)

523 _____. "The Empress of Morocco: a Critical Edition of the Play and the Controversy Surrounding It." Doctoral Dissertation: University of Illinois, 1963. 685pp.

Doyle identifies the sections of Notes and Observations "that seem most conclusively Dryden's, pointing out verbal and critical parallels between this and Dryden's other works."

524 Love, H. R. R. "The Authorship of the Postscript of Notes and Observations on The Empress of Morocco," N&Q, XIII (1966), 27-8.

Argues that Shadwell wrote it.

525 Novak, Maximillian E. The Empress of Morocco and Its Critics. Los Angeles: William Andrews Clark Memorial Library, University of California, 1968. 358pp.

Reviewed by Geoffrey Marshall in SCN, XXVIII, 70-2.

Of Dramatic Poesy: an Essay (1668): (see also #516)

526 Adam, Donald Geikie. "John Dryden: a Study of His Prose Achievement." Doctoral Dissertation: University of Rochester, 1963. 226pp.

Adam provides "a survey of his prose works, a description of them, and an analysis of Dryden's characteristic usages," with attention to the Essay.

527 Aden, John M. "Dryden, Corneille, and the Essay of Dramatic Poesy," RES, VI (1955), 147-56.

Finds that the examen device comes from Corneille but not the Essay's structure, and states that Corneille"s influence is limited to "commonplaces and miscellaneous fragments of dramatic history, contemporary French politics, and dramatic techniques."

528 Archer, Stanley. "The Persons in An Essay of Dramatic Poesy," PLL, II (1966), 305-14.

Finds that the characterizations very closely resemble their real-life models.

529 Bately, Janet M. "Dryden and Branded Words," N&Q, XII (1965), 134-9.

Examines vocabulary changes in the second edition of the Essay, 1684.

530 _____. "Dryden's Revisions in the Essay of Dramatic Poesy: the Preposition at the End of the Sentence and the Expression of the Relative," RES, XV (1964), 268-82.

Illustrates a general fluctuation in usage.

531 Cooke, Arthur L. "Did Dryden hear the Guns?" N&Q, CXCVI 204-5.

Dates the battle, June 3, 1665, and substantiates Dryden's claim that the Essay's party did hear the guns.

532 Davie, Donald A. "Dramatic Poetry: Dryden's Conversation-Piece," CamJ, V (1952), 553-61.

Considers the Essay more interesting as a conversation-piece than as criticism.

533 Hemphill, George. "Dryden's Heroic Line," PMLA, LXXII (1957), 863-79.

Examines Dryden's metrics in the context of some statements in the Essay.

534 Huntley, Frank L. On Dryden's Essay of Dramatic Poesy. (The University of Michigan Contributions in Modern Philology, 16.) Ann Arbor: University of Michigan Press, 1951. vii + 71pp.

Analyzes the Essay's argument and significance, and finds that the theories are repeated in later essays. Reviewed by H. Kossmann in ES, XXXIII, 269-70; by Pierre Legouis in EA, V, 359; and, by Samuel Holt Monk in PQ, XXXI, 269-70.

535 Jauslin, Christian. "John Dryden's Essay of Dramatic Poesy, 1668," Schweitzer Monatschefte, XLVIII (1968), 215-21.

Examines the historical context and critical positions of the Essay.

536 Jones, H. W. "Some, Further Pope-Dryden Indebtedness?"

N&Q, CXCVIII (1953), 199-200.

Notes parallels involving Pope's **Essay on Criticism** and **An Epistle to Dr. Arbuthnot** and Dryden's **Essay**.

537 Jones, Richard Foster. "Science and Criticism in the Neo-Classical Age of English Literature," **The Seventeenth Century: Studies in the History of English Thought from Bacon to Pope**. Stanford: Stanford University Press, 1951. Pp. 41-74, esp. 44-9.

Suggests that Dryden was inspired by scientific progress.

538 Kaplan, Charles. "Dryden's **An Essay of Dramatic Poesy**," Exp, VIII (1950), #36.

Notes that Dryden accomplished his general purpose "to vindicate the honour of our English writers from the censure of those who unjustly prefer the French before them."

539 Kirsch, Arthur C. "An Essay on **Dramatic Poetry**, (1681)," HLQ, XXVIII (1964), 89-91.

Discusses an essay which praises Dryden as a dramatist.

540 LeClercq, Richard V. "The Academic Nature of the Whole Discourse of **An Essay of Dramatic Poesy**," PLL, VIII (1972), 27-38.

Distinguishes between 'pyrrhonism' and 'academic reasoning' and argues that Ciceronian doctrine and method "figure significantly" in Dryden's "'Preface' to Buckhurst as well as the dialogue itself."

541 _____. "Corneille and **An Essay of Dramatic Poesy**," CL, XXII (1970), 319-27.

Assigns to the Frenchman "the crucial role in proving the judiciousness of the English argument and in making possible Dryden's claim to Socratic scepticism."

542 _____. "John Dryden: **An Essay of Dramatic Poesy**." Doctoral Dissertation: University of California at Los Angeles, 1968. 299pp.

On the text, real-life models, the critical milieu, and the Platonism of the **Essay**.

543 Leeman, Richard Kendall. "Corneille and Dryden: Their Theories of Dramatic Poetry." Doctoral Dissertation:

The University of Wisconsin, 1961.

Illustrates that the two were similarly independent of neo-Aristotelian principles, such as those governing memesis and dramatic purpose.

544 Loftis, John. "Dryden's Criticism of Spanish Drama," The Augustan Milieu: Essays Presented to Louis A. Landa. Edited by Henry Knight Miller, Eric Rothstein, and G. S. Rousseau. Oxford: The Clarendon Press; New York: Oxford University Press, 1970. Pp. 18-31.

Argues that Dryden's references to Spanish drama in the Essay are "ambivalent or deprecatory" and concludes that "Spanish and French drama sometimes represent in Dryden's writings a schematic antithesis: drama of action, exciting perhaps, but diffuse, and drama of character, sometimes tedius, but orderly and at best concentrated and moving."

545 McNamara, Peter. "Clothing Thought: Dryden on Language," TSE, XX (1972), 57-70.

Examines the idea that language is the dress of thought and notes Dryden's linguistic openmindedness.

546 Mace, Dean C. "Dryden's Dialogue on Drama," JWCI, XXV (1962), 87-112.

Argues that the essay is "an examen" with the aims "of discovering whatever truths may belong to dramatic criticism and showing their foundation in nature."

547 Miner, Earl. "Renaissance Contexts of Dryden's Criticism," MQR, XII (Spring, 1973), 97-115.

Festschriften: "Essays Presented to Frank Livingston Huntley," edited by Russell Fraser. Miner compares Dryden's Essay of Dramatic Poesy with Sir Philip Sidney's Apology for Poesy, arguing that Dryden's criticism shows we can know ourselves through literature.

548 Pollon, Burton R. "'The World is too Much With Us': two Sources--Dryden and Godwin," WC, I (1970), 50-2.

549 "Dryden's Essay of Dramatic Poesy," Exp, XIII (1955), #46.

On the scope of the dialogue and atmosphere of the opening scene.

550 Schulz, Max F. "Coleridge's 'Debt' to Dryden and Johnson," N&Q, X (1963), 189-91.

Coleridge, Johnson, and Dryden on the metaphysical poets.

551 Simon, Irène. "Dryden's Revision of the Essay of Dramatic Poesy," RES, XIV (1963), 132-41.

Finds that the 1684 edition is more colloquial.

552 Singh, Sarup. "Dryden and the Unities," IJES, II (1961), 78-90.

Defends the age of Dryden against Robert Graves' charge of obsequiousness.

553 Strang, Barbara M. H. "Dryden's Innovations in Critical Vocabulary," DUJ, LI (1959), 114-23.

Her purpose is "to define Dryden's contribution to a particular range of expression in English, and to adjust current notions about the resources of the language at a particular period."

554 Swedenberg, H. T., Jr. "Dryden's Obsessive Concern with the Heroic," SP (Extra Series, Jan., 1967), 12-26.

Examines epic theory in the non-dramatic works.

555 Tave, Stuart M. "Corbyn Morris; Falstaff, Humor, and Comic Theory in the Eighteenth Century," ML, L (1952), 102-15.

Focusses on the discussion of Falstaff in the Essay.

556 Thale, Mary. "Dryden's Dramatic Criticism: Polestar of the Ancients," CL, XVIII (1966), 36-54.

Discusses the variations in Dryden's interpretations of classical theorists, noting his concept of the imitation of nature.

557 ———. "The Framework of An Essay of Dramatic Poesy," PLL, VIII (1972), 362-9.

Conjectures that Dryden delayed the publication of the Essay in order to counter the mood of national retrogression, and examines the relationship of "art and patriotism" in the work.

558 Tillyard, E. M. W. "A Note on Dryden's Criticism," The Seventeenth Century: Studies in the History of English Thought and Literature from Bacon to Pope. Stanford: Stanford University Press, 1951. Pp. 330-8.

Traces the development of Dryden's critical tone, noting an early formality in the Essay.

559 Tyson, Gerald. "Dryden's Dramatic Essay," Ar, IV (1973), 72-85.

"Of Heroic Plays: an Essay," prefixed to The Conquest of Granada by the Spaniards, in Two Parts (1672):

560 Hume, Robert D. "Dryden on Creation: 'Imagination' in the Later Criticism," RES, XXI (1970), 295-314.

Argues that Dryden's statements on the creative imagination must be measured against his lifelong belief that "literary criticism depends in large part on a 'craft' and correction which demands the extensive application of judgement to the products of the inventive and aggregative faculties."

"Preface of the Translator, with a Parallel of Poetry and Painting," prefixed to De arte graphica: the Art of Painting, by C. A. du Fresnoy (1695):

561 Monk, Samuel H. "Dryden's 'Eminent French Critic' in A Parallel of Poetry and Painting," N&Q, II (1955), 433.

Identifies the critic as André Dacier.

"Preface" to Fables Ancient and Modern, Translated into Verse from Homer, Ovid, Boccace, and Chaucer, with Original Poems (1700):

562 Cole, Elmer J., Jr. "The Consistency of John Dryden's Literary Criticism in Theory and Practice," Doctoral Dissertation: The University of New Mexico, 1970. 155pp.

Cole finds that "The fundamental point is that his personal tastes were grounded firmly on principle. He defends his preference for Chaucer over Ovid, Shakespeare over Fletcher, Juvenal over Horace, and Homer over Virgil, on solid and consistent neoclassical theory, as well as on his own individual reactions."

563 Sherwood, John C. "Dryden and the Rules: the Preface to the *Fables*," JEGP, LII (1953), 13-26.

>Holds that "the great merit in Dryden is not as some think that he could escape from the rules, but rather that he can apply them with reasonableness and common sense and that he could keep his eyes on the essentials."

"Preface, the Grounds of Criticism in Tragedy," prefixed to *Troilus and Cressida* (1679):

564 Rothstein, Eric. "English Tragic Theory in the Late Seventeenth Century," ELH, XXIX (1962), 306-23.

>Discusses the preface to *Troilus and Cressida* and *Heads of an Answer to Rymer's Remarks on the Tragedies of the Last Age* as documents which contain the "fabulist" and "affective" positions of Dryden.

565 Sherwood, John C. "Dryden and the Rules: the Preface to *Troilus and Cressida*," CL, II (1950), 73-83.

>Examines its "orthodox" French neo-classical principles and calls it one of Dryden's best essays.

On Prose Style

566 Aden, John M. "Dryden and Saint Evremond," CL, VI (1954), 232-9.

>Points out "fundamental differences" between Dryden and Saint Evremond.

567 Adolph, Robert. *The Rise of Modern Prose Style*. Cambridge, Mass., and London: The M. I. T. Press, 1968. Pp. 220-6.

>Finds Dryden "updating Bacon's writing in *Methods*, which has its origin in the utilitarian requirement of persuasive and useful discourse."

568 Bady, David Michael. "The Exact Balance of True Virtue: John Dryden and the Tradition of Epideictic Comparison." Doctoral Dissertation: Columbia University, 1972. 500pp.

Studies "the author who perhaps most thoroughly immersed himself in the culture of comparison was the deliberate rhetorician, John Dryden. Not only those of his works clearly associated with epideixis, the dedications and ceremonial poems, but also his criticism, and even such apparently autonomous creations as the heroic plays, are meant to be read as syncrises."

569 Brown, David D. "John Tillotson's Revisions and Dryden's 'Talent for English Prose,'" RES, XII (1961), 24-39.

Discusses Tillotson's Sermons and Wisdom of Being Religious, suggests that Dryden may have seen them in manuscript, and conjectures that they may have provided models.

570 Butt, John. "A Plea for More English Dictionaries," DUJ, XLIII (1951), 96-102.

Discusses briefly Dryden's usage and vocabulary, and calls for a seventeenth century dictionary, which would show Dryden's potential scope. Reprinted in Butt's Pope, Dickens, and Others; Essays and Addresses (Edinburgh, 1969).

571 Dobrée, Bonamy. "Dryden's Prose," in #156 above, pp. 171-88.

Examines the concern with language, noting Matthew Arnold's statement that Dryden wrote "the true English Prose."

572 Feder, Lillian. "John Dryden's Use of Classical Rhetoric," PMLA, LXIX (1954), 1258-78.

Examines the influence of Cicero and Quintillian. Reprinted in #177 above, 493-518.

573 Hamilton, K. G. "Dryden and Seventeenth Century Prose Style," in #167 above, pp. 297-324.

Analyzes "Dryden's prose style in its seventeenth century context . . . both of ideas about prose style and of actual practice."

574 Read, Herbert. English Prose Style. Boston: Beacon Press, 1952. Pp. 104, 185-6, 192-4.

575 Simon, Irène. "Dryden's Prose Style," RLV, XXXI (1965), 506-28.

Finds that it is "slightly formalized everyday speech adapted to a specific audience." Reprinted in Stanley

E. Fish, ed., Seventeenth Century Prose: Modern Essays in Criticism (New York, 1971).

576 Smith, Harold Wendell. "Nature, Correctness, and Decorum," Scrutiny, XVIII (1952), 287-314.

   Notes that "Dryden uses language as a tailor uses cloth" and finds a "safe separation of abstract from concrete, thought from 'sensory' experience or sensation, 'thoughts' from words, manner from matter, 'reason' from 'its slaves the passions,'" in Dryden's prose.

577 Söderlind, Johannes. Verb Syntax in John Dryden's Prose. 2 vols. (Essays and Studies in English Language and Literature, 19.) Cambridge, Mass.: Harvard University Press; Uppsala: A.-B. Lundeqviska Bokhandeln, 1951, 1958.

   Vol. I reviewed by F. Mossé in EA, V, 70; and by A. A. Hill in SLing, X, 84-7; Vol. II reviewed by Karl Brunner in Anglia, LXXVIII, 499-500; and Ewald Standop in Archiv, CXCVI, 213; both vols. reviewed by R. W. Zandvoort in ES, XLVII, 304-6.

578 Williamson, George. The Senecan Amble: a Study in Prose Form from Bacon to Collier. Chicago: University of Chicago Press, 1951. Pp. 301-35.

   An examination of Dryden's ascendancy to the position of "master of the new prose."

VI POETRY:

Comprehensive and Miscellaneous Studies

579 Adams, Percy G. "'Harmony of Numbers': Dryden's Alliteration, Consonance, Assonance," TSLL, IX (1967), 333-43.

   Argues that Dryden aimed for "a sonorous, reinforcing antithesis," and an affective "modification in the reader."

580 Anthony, Geraldine Marie. "Divine Imagery in Dryden's Lyric Poetry." Doctoral Dissertation: St. John's University, 1963.

581 Baker, Van Roy. "Dryden's Military Imagery." Doctoral

Dissertation: Columbia University, 1968. 218pp.

Examines all the works but the translations.

582 Barnes, T. R. English Verse: Voice and Movement from Wyatt to Yeats. Cambridge: Cambridge University Press, 1967. x + 324pp.

A study of the sounds of poetry with numerous references to Dryden.

583 Beall, Chandler B. "A Quaint Conceit from Guarini to Dryden," MLN, LXIV (1949), 461-8.

'Die'

584 Blair, Joel Mac, Jr. "Dryden and Fanciful Poetry." Doctoral Dissertation: Harvard University, 1965.

585 _____. "Dryden's Ceremonial Hero," SEL, IX (1969), 379-93.

Finds that "changing faces of a single poetic character" appear in Dryden's early poems, serving "a ritualistic or ceremonial function."

586 Brett, Richard David. "Ironic Harmony: Poetic Structure in Donne, Marvell, and Dryden." Doctoral Dissertation: Cornell University, 1961. 347pp.

Brett contrasts the styles of Donne and Marvell with Dryden's, "whose neo-classicism is in almost direct opposition to the metaphysical" poets.

587 Brinkley, Roberta Florence. Coleridge on the Seventeenth Century. Durham: Duke University Press, 1955; New York: Greenwood Press, Publishers, 1968. Pp. 630-3, 679.

Excerpts from Coleridge's prose on Dryden's poetry and drama.

588 Brower, Reuben A. "Dryden and the 'Invention' of Pope," Restoration and Eighteenth Century Literature: Essays in Honor of Alan Dugald McKillop. Chicago and London: The University of Chicago Press; Toronto: The University of Toronto Press, 1963. Pp. 211-33.

Discusses Dryden's pastoral and descriptive modes and his relaxed, personal, colloquial Horatian style.

589 Davison, Dennis. Dryden. (Literature in Perspective

Series.) London: Evans Brothers, Ltd., 1968. 151pp.

Background and analysis of the poems. Davison holds that "Dryden's rococo finery has a steel framework of earnest concern for man and society." Reviewed by Ted-Larry Pebworth in SCN, XXXI, #3.

590 Dobrée, Bonamy. "Dryden's Poems," Sew Rev, LXVII (1964), 519-26.

Discusses Dryden's poetry in a review of #3 above.

591 Emslie, McD. "Dryden's Couplets: Imagery Vowed to Poverty," CritQ, II (1960), 51-7.

Maintains that the imagery subordinates content to rhetoric, hence, vowed to a poverty of meaning.

592 _____. "Dryden's Couplets: Wit and Conversation," EIC, XI (1961), 264-73.

A discussion of tone and attitude.

593 Erskine-Hill, Howerd. "John Dryden: the Poet and Critic," Dryden to Johnson. Edited by E. R. Lonsdale. London: Barrie & Jenkins, 1971. Pp. 23-59.

594 Evans, Betty Douglas. "Dryden's Imagery in His Non-Dramatic Poetry." Doctoral Dissertation: University of Oklahoma, 1957. 374pp.

Concludes that "Dryden believed imagery must suit not only the genre and level of style but also the subject-matter and tone of the poem."

595 Freedman, Morris. "Dryden's Reported Reaction to Paradise Lost," N&Q, V (1958), 14-16.

Doubts the stories that Dryden admired Milton's blank verse.

596 _____. "Milton and Dryden on Rhyme," HLQ, XXIV (1961), 337-44.

Argues that Milton's attack on rhyme in the preface to Paradise Lost was likely the result of his publisher's insistence that he engage in the Dryden-Howard controversy on rhyme on drama.

597 Geis, Walter. "Die Anschauungen von den religiosen und politischen Ordnungen in der Dichtung John Drydens: Dargestellt vornehmlich auf Grund der Interpretation

der Lehrgedichte im Zusammenhang des Gesamtwerkes."
Doctoral Dissertation: Universität Frankfurt A/M, 1950.

598   Golladay, Gertrude Ledean. "The Rhetorical Poetic Tradition in Dryden's Two Verse Essays." Doctoral Dissertation: Texas Christian University, 1968.

599   Hamilton, Kenneth Gordon. John Dryden and the Poetry of Statement. St. Lucia, Brisbane: University of Queensland Press, 1967; East Lansing: Michigan State University Press, 1969. 193pp.

Reviewed by Pierre Legouis in EA, XXI, 308-9.

600   Hart, Jeffrey. "John Dryden: the Politics of Style," MA, VIII (1964), 399-408.

Argues that Dryden's "subordination of metaphor and conceit" indicates "attitudes that go beyond the writing of verse, and that involve the deepest questions of politics and morals."

601   Highet, Gilbert. The Classical Tradition: Greek and Roman Influences on Western Literature. Oxford: The Clarendon Press; New York: Oxford University Press, 1949. xxxviii + 763pp.

Scattered short notes on several poems place them in the context of their classical backgrounds and lines of development.

602   Kermode, Frank. "The Poet and His Public--Dryden: a 'Poet's Poet,'" Listener, LVII (1957), 877-8.

603   Kinsley, J. "Diction and Style in the Poetry of John Dryden." Doctoral Dissertation: University of Edinburgh, 1951.

604   _____. "Dryden and the 'Encomium Musicae,'" RES, IV (1953), 263-7.

Applies the Renaissance theory that music expands, contracts, and tranquillizes the soul to Dryden's poetry.

605   Knights, L. C. Public Voices: Literature and Politics with Special Reference to the Seventeenth Century. (Clark Lectures for 1970-71.) London: Chatto & Windus, Ltd., 1971. 134pp.

Discusses Dryden as a "simplifier" and "purveyor of abstractions," and as one "whose rhetoric obfuscates interpretation and clear statement."

606 Legouis, Pierre. "Ouvrages Récents sur Dryden," EA, XVII (1964), 148-58.

Reviews #s 37, 114, 120, 141, 153 above, and 842 below.

607 Leyburn, Ellen Douglass. Satiric Allegory: Mirror of Man. (Yale Studies in English, 130.) New Haven: Yale University Press, 1956; Hamden, Conn.: Archon Books, 1969. Pp. 15-22, 34-7.

Places Dryden's use of allegory in a continuum from Erasmus to the twentieth century, and focusses on Absalom and Achitophel and MacFlecknoe.

608 Masson, David I. "Dryden's Phonetic Rhetoric: Some Passages from His Original Poems," PLPLSLHS, XI (1964), 1-5.

609 Miner, Earl. Dryden's Poetry. Bloomington and London: Indiana University Press, 1967. xxii + 354pp.

Bibliography, 327-34. Includes a chapter on All for Love. Miner characterizes the poetry in the word 'harmony': "It conveys a unity achieved from highly diverse elements, a concept of order which is dynamic rather than fixed, and, as the poems upon music reveal, a symbol of creative energy." Reviewed by Eugene M. Waith in YR, LVII, 123-6; by Reuben A. Brower in MLQ, XXIX, 110-12; by Arthur W. Hoffman in MP, LXVI, 166-8; by John C. Sherwood in CL, XXI, 277-80; and, in TLS, Jan. 9, 1969, 41.

610 Miner, Earl. "Forms and Motive of Narrative Poetry," in #168 above, pp. 234-66.

Holds that "No other English poet has Dryden's obsession with, or power over, that form of analogy more sustained than syntactic metaphor but less strict than allegory."

611 Morgan, Edwin. "Dryden's Drudging," CamJ, VI (1953), 414-29.

Assesses Dryden's literary achievement within his literary milieu. Reprinted in #172 above, 55-70.

612 Murakami, Shikō. "Reverence for Human Nature: the Poetry of Dryden and Pope," Journal of the Faculty of Letters, Osaka University, X (1963), i-vi, 1-84.

613 Murphree, A. A. "Wit and Dryden," All These to Teach: Essays in Honor of C. A. Robertson. Edited by Robert

A. Bryan, Alton C. Morris, A. A. Murphree, and Aubrey L. Williams. Gainesville: University of Florida Press, 1965. Pp. 159-70.

614　Piper, William Bowman. The Heroic Couplet. Cleveland and London: The Press of Case Western Reserve University, 1969. Pp. 99-118.

Examines metrics in political and later poetry.

615　Price, Martin. To the Palace of Wisdom: Studies in Order and Energy from Dryden to Blake. Garden City: Doubleday & Company, Inc., 1964. Pp. 28-78.

Illustrates the dialectical nature of Dryden's poetry.

616　Prince, F. T. "Dryden Redivivus," RES, I (1960), 71-9.

Discusses the poetry in a review of #3 above.

617　Ramsey, Paul. The Art of John Dryden. Lexington: University of Kentucky Press, 1969. x + 214pp.

On metrics and poetic principles with a chapter on All for Love. Reviewed by John M. Aden in SAB, XXXV, 66-8; and by William Frost in JEGP, LXX, 310-12.

618　Reaske, Christopher. Monarch Literature Notes on the Poetry of Dryden. New York: Monarch Press, 1965. 123pp. (Bibliography, 120-3.)

619　Rivers, Isabel. "The Poetry of Conservatism, 1600-1745: Jonson, Dryden, and Pope." Doctoral Dissertation: Columbia University, 1969. 407pp.

Relates the three on the point "of their public poetic function and . . . the challenging of this function by the course of political events."

620　Roper, Alan Henry. "Dryden and the Stuart Succession." Doctoral Dissertation: The Johns Hopkins University, 1961.

621　Sinclair, Giles Merten. "The Aesthetic Function of Rime in Dryden's Verse." Doctoral Dissertation: The University of Michigan, 1953.

Argues that "an evaluation of rime must take into account the meanings of the rime words as well as their sounds and consider their relationship to the verse units in which they occur, both in meaning and sound."

622 Soule, George Alan, Jr. "Dryden and the Poetry of Public Action." Doctoral Dissertation: Yale University, 1960.

623 Spencer, Jeffry Burress. "Five Poetic Landscapes, 1650-1750. Heroic and Ideal Landscape in English Poetry from Marvell to Thomson." Doctoral Dissertation: Northwestern University, 1971. 473pp.

Relates Dryden to Milton on the point of "the classical baroque," and to Pope and Thomson in "knowledge of the visual arts."

624 Sutherland, James R. John Dryden: the Poet as Orator. (The Twentieth W. P. Ker Memorial Lecture Delivered in the University of Glasgow, 21st February, 1962.) Glasgow: Jackson, 1963. 29pp.

Reviewed in TLS, March 19, 1963, 241.

625 Thale, Mary. "Dryden's Unwritten Epic," PLL, V (1969), 423-33.

Discusses Dryden's "inability to adapt the epic theory and practice of the ancients," noting that his plays were influenced by classical rules and practice.

626 Vieth, David M. "Concept as Metaphor: Dryden's Attempted Stylistic Revolution," LS, III (1970), 197-204.

627 Wallace, John M. "Dryden and History: a Problem in Allegorical Reading," ELH, XXXVI (1969), 265-90.

Holds that Dryden's historizing was more than "merely a metaphorical account of recent events with an implied moral," noting that he depended upon the reader to extrapolate.

628 Wedgwood, C. V. Seventeenth Century English Literature. (The Home University Library of Modern Knowledge, 218.) London and New York: Oxford University Press, 1950. Pp. 128-35.

Notes that Dryden belongs "wholly to the troubled and passionate seventeenth century."

629 Williamson, George. The Proper Wit of Poetry. Chicago: The University of Chicago Press; London: Faber and Faber, Ltd.; Toronto: The University of Toronto Press, 1961. Pp. 84-134.

Examines Dryden's theory and practice concerning the "problem" left him by his literary predecessors: "the regulation of wit."

630 Woods, Thomas Francis. "Dryden and the Prophetic Mode: an Examination of His Poetic Theory and Practice in Light of Seventeenth-Century Concepts of Prophecy." Doctoral Dissertation: The Ohio State University, 1973,

Finds that "Dryden was knowledgeable about both millenarianism and prophecy; throughout his career he considered using the prophetic in poetry; his poems contain devices of language closely resembling those defined as prophetic by contemporary exegetes; and he wrote major poems that are coherent and powerful when read as prophetic."

631 Zwicker, Steven Nathan. "Dryden and the Sacred History of the English People: a Study of Typological Imagery In Dryden's Political Poetry, 1660-1688." Doctoral Dissertation: Brown University, 1969. 298pp.

Examines Dryden's "repeated attempts to see men and events of his own day in terms of the sacred history of the biblical past." (See #697 below.)

On the Elegies:

comprehensive study

632 Williams, David W. "The Funeral Elegies of John Dryden." Doctoral Dissertation: Yale University, 1972. 223pp.

on specific elegies:

Eleanora: a Panegyrical Poem Dedicated to the Memory of the Late Countess of Abingdon (1692):

633 Benson, Donald R. "Platonism and Neoclassic Metaphor: Dryden's Eleanora and Donne's Anniversaries," SP, LXVIII (1971), 340-56.

Asks "what manner of Platonism underlies Dryden's metaphor, and how does it relate to the undoubted Neo-Platonism underlying Donne's."

To the Memory of Mr. Oldham (1674):

634   Bache, William B. "Dryden and Oldham: Hail and Farewell," CLAJ, XII (1969), 237-43.

      Maintains "the poem is more nearly about Dryden than it is about Oldham."

635   Clark, John R. "To the Memory of Mr. Oldham: Dryden's Disquieting Lines," CP, III (1970), 43-9.

      Notes "jarring antitheses, paradoxes, and untenable positions."

636   Freedman, Morris. "Milton and Dryden." Doctoral Dissertation: Columbia University, 1953. 207pp.

      States that "Dryden began moving away from Milton with his elegy to Oldham, which was written in the same genre as Lycidas, and marked a conscientious giving up by Dryden of the vigorous Miltonic manner of the satires."

637   King, Bruce. "Lycidas and Oldham," EA, XIX (1966), 60-3.

      Discusses parallels and notes that Oldham is the more classical poem.

638   Mell, Donald Charles. "Variations on Elegiac Themes: Dryden, Pope, Prior, Gray, Johnson." Doctoral Dissertation: University of Pennsylvania, 1961. 241pp.

      Shows "how Dryden develops his dual themes of praise and literary criticism by combining diction, sound, metaphor, and allusion in the form of a classical elegy."

639   Moscovit, Leonard. "An Echo of Gellius in Dryden's Oldham," N&Q, XIX (1972), 26-7.

      From Noctes Atticae, XIII, ii, 3-6.

640   Parkin, Rebecca Price. "The Journey Down the Great Scale Reflected in Two Neoclassical Elegies," EE, I (1970), 197-204.

      A historiographic reading of Dryden's poem and Johnson's On the Death of Dr. Robert Levet, noting a downward progression in both.

641   Peterson, R. G. "The Unavailing Gift: Dryden's Roman Farewell to Mr. Oldham," MP, LXVI (1969), 232-6.

Discusses the influence of Catullus, 101, on the poem.

To the Pious Memory of the Accomplisht Young Lady Mrs Anne Killigrew, Excellent in the two Sister-Arts of Poësie, and Painting. An Ode (1686):

642 Eleanor, Mother Mary, S.H.C.J. "Anne Killigrew and Mac-Flecknoe," PQ, XLIII (1964), 47-54.

Compares the imagery of these two "treatments of a single theme--the fall and restoration of poetry."

643 Heath-Stubbs, John. "Baroque Ceremony: a Study of Dryden's Ode to the Memory of Mistress Anne Killigrew (1686)," CSE, III (1959), 76-84.

644 Hoffman, Arthur W. "Note on a Dryden Ode," TLS, June 19, 1959, 369.

Notes that the lamp of Epictetus image refers to Lucian's The Ignorant Book-Collector.

645 Hope, A. D. "Anne Killigrew, or the Art of Modulating," Illustrates how Dryden maintains "the tone of the poem as a whole, while modulating skillfully from one level to another," as in music. Reprinted in #156 above, 99-113; and in Hope's The Cave in the Spring (Adelaide, 1965), 129-43.

646 Jerome, Judson. "On Decoding Humor," AnR, XX (Winter, 1960-1), 479-93, esp. 486-7.

Notes that a kind of humor modifies "the quite sincere grief," in Anne Killigrew.

647 Shawcross, John T. "Some Literary Uses of Numerology," HSL, I (1969), 50-62, esp. 54-9.

Contends that "the artifact of numerological mysticism has dictated the subject matter and development of Dryden's ode."

648 Vieth, David M. "Irony in Dryden's Ode to Anne Killigrew," SP, LXII (1965), 91-100.

Examines phrasing, imagery, and tone to support the thesis that there is a gentle irony in the portrait of the woman.

Upon the Death of Lord Hastings (1649):

649   Aden, John M. "Shakespeare in Dryden's First Published Poem," N&Q, II (1955), 22-3.

   Argues that the débat scenes in Hamlet, apparent in lines 9-12 of Dryden's poem, suggest a very early Shakespearean influence.

650   Hughes, Richard. "John Dryden's Upon the Death of the Lord Hastings: Royalist Polemic," Greyfriar, VII (1964), 13-19.

651   Milburn, D. Judson. The Age of Wit, 1650-1750. New York: The Macmillan Company; London: Collier-Macmillan, Ltd., 1966. Pp. 69-77.

   Illustrates that Hastings "depends heavily upon the rhetoric of wit, reflecting the continuing manner of conceit of metaphysical poetry."

652   Ringler, Richard N. "Two Dryden Notes," ELN, I (June, 1964), Pp. 256-61.

   Traces the Sphere of Archimedes image to Claudian.

653   Wallerstein, Ruth. Studies in Seventeenth Century Poetic. Madison: University of Wisconsin Press, 1950. Pp. 115-142.

654   Wilson, Gayle E. "Genre and Rhetoric in Dryden's Upon the Death of the Lord Hastings," SSJ, XXXV (1970), 256-66.

   This analysis of Hastings shows Dryden's indebtedness to the classical theory of decorum, modifies the charges of insincerity, and illustrates Dryden's preoccupation with ancient rhetoricians.

Epistles in Verse

comprehensive studies

655   Mace, Agnes K. "The Public Verse Epistle from Dryden to Burns." Doctoral Dissertation: The Catholic University of America, 1954. 185pp.

656   Moore, Charles Arthur. "The Familiar Verse Epistle from

Dryden to Pope." Doctoral Dissertation: University of
Oregon, 1970. 187pp.

Finds that Dryden "combines purposes to develop the
didactic-complimentary epistle."

on specific epistles

<u>Lines to Mrs. Creed</u> (?):

657 Sweney, John R. "Dryden's <u>Lines to Mrs. Creed</u>," PQ, LI
(1972), 489-90.

Notes that the emendations for the 1800 edition were
based on Malone's annotated copy of his <u>Life of Dryden</u>.

<u>To My Dear Friend Mr. Congreve, on His Comedy, call'd The
Double Dealer</u> (1694):

658 Hoffman, Arthur W. "Dryden's <u>To Mr. Congreve</u>," MLN,
LXXV (1960), 553-6.

Discusses the "architectural metaphors" in lines 15-19,
noting Dryden's dislike for the work of Sir Christopher
Wren.

<u>To My Honour'd Friend, Dr. Charleton, on his learned and useful Works; and more particularly this of STONE-HENG, by him Restored to the true Founders</u> (1663):

659 Cameron, Allen Barry. "Donne and Dryden: Their Achievement in the Verse Epistle," Discourse, II (1968), 252-6.

Compares <u>To Sir Henry Wotton</u> with Dryden's poem, and
finds that Dryden's is political and unified.

660 Golden, Samuel A. "Dryden's Praise of Dr. Charleton,"
Hermathena, CIII (1966), 59-65.

661 _____. "Dryden's <u>To My Honored Friend, Dr. Charleton</u>," Exp, XXIV (1966), #53.

Notes a pun on stones: medical and on Stonehenge.

662 Wasserman, Earl R. "Dryden's Epistle to Charleton," JEGP, LV (1956), 201-12.

　　On the political "status of the crown" in the poem.

663 ──────. The Subtler Language: Critical Readings of Neoclassic and Romantic Poems. Baltimore: Johns Hopkins Press, 1959. Pp. 15-44.

　　Examines Dryden's focus on Charles II and the Danes. Reprinted as "Dryden: Epistle to Charleton," in #172 above, 71-85.

To My Honoured Friend, Sir ROBERT HOWARD, On his Excellent Poems (1660):

664 Johnson, James William. "Dryden's Epistle to Robert Howard," BSUF, II (1961), 20-4.

　　Examines the contributions of structure and tone toward thematic content.

665 Vieth, David M. "Irony in Dryden's Verses to Sir Robert Howard," EIC, XXII (1972), 239-43.

　　Finds that irony in the poem, evident in the lines praising Howard's translations of Virgil and Statius, is subordinated to "gentlemanly commendation."

To My Honour'd Kinsman, JOHN DRIDEN, OF CHESTERTON IN THE COUNTY OF HUNTINGDON, ESQUIRE (1700):

666 Hibbard, G. R. "The Country House Poem of the Seventeenth Century," JWCI, XIX (1956), 159-77, esp. pt. vii.

　　Concludes that Dryden had no "true understanding of country life or feeling for it."

667 Levine, Jay Arnold. "John Dryden's Epistle to John Driden," JEGP, LXIII (1964), 450-74.

　　Examines the three subjects of the poem: Dryden, England, and Driden, concluding that the poem documents the poet's state of affairs in 1700.

To Sir Godfrey Kneller (1694):

668 Guibbory, Achsah. "Dryden's Views of History," PQ, LII (1973), 187-204.

669 Levine, Jay Arnold. "The Status of the Verse Epistle Before Pope," SP, LIX (1962), 658-84, esp. pt. iii.

   Discusses Dryden's meaningful use of the addressee.

670 Miner, Earl. "Dryden's 'Eikon Basilike': To Sir Godfrey Kneller," Seventeenth-Century Imagery: Essays on Uses of Figurative Language from Donne to Farquhar. Edited by Earl Miner. Berkeley, Los Angeles, and London: University of California Press, 1971. Pp. 151-67.

   Focusses on Dryden's concept of the poet-king. Miner states that "The poem is pessimistic about the present but optimistic about the future, when Time will restore art to its proper position and the artist-king to his just place."

The Miscellanies

671 Roberts, William. "Saint-Amant, Orinda, and Dryden's Miscellany," ELN, I (March, 1964), 191-6.

   States that the poem on solitude in the fourth issue of the Dryden-Tonson Miscellany, Vol. I, 1716, 1727, is based on "La Solitude de St. Amant English'd," in Katherine Philips' Poems, 1667.

The Odes

On the Marriage of the Fair and Vertuous Lady, Mrs. Anastasia Stafford, with that Truly Worthy and Pious Gent. George Holman, Esq. A Pindarique Ode (?, published 1813):

672 Miner, Earl. "Dryden's Ode on Mrs. Anastasia Stafford," HLQ, XXX (1967), 103-11.

   Discusses the poem's discovery, historical background, and place in the canon.

St. Cecilia's Day odes

dual studies

673 Davies, H. Neville. "Dryden and Vossius: a Reconsideration," JWCI, XXIX (1966), 282-95.

Holds that Dryden was not influenced by the theory of 'rhythmus' in the odes, and discusses Dryden's statements concerning the relationship of words and music. This article disagrees with #677 below. (Cf. Mace's "A Reply to Mr. H. Neville Davies's 'Dryden and Vossius: a Reconsideration," JWCI, XXIX, 296-310.)

674 Heath-Stubbs, John. The Ode. London: Oxford University Press, 1969. Pp. 42-8.

675 Hollander, John. The Untuning of the Sky: Ideas of Music in English Poetry, 1500-1700. Princeton: Princeton University Press, 1961. Pp. 401-32.

Examines the odes, noting that "Before Dryden the Patroness of music tended to receive only passing mention." Reprinted as "The Odes to Music," in #172 above, 149-64.

676 MacCubbin, Robert Purks. "A Critical Study of Odes for St. Cecilia's Day, 1683-1697." Doctoral Dissertation: University of Illinois, 1969. 249pp.

Studies "Dryden's ethic concerning the function of the mimetic artist in a fallen world full, symbolically, of 'grating consonants and shifting rhythms.'"

677 Mace, D. T. "Musical Humanism, the Doctrine of Rhythmus and the Saint Cecilia Odes of Dryden," JWCI, XXVII (1964), 251-92.

Argues that Renaissance modes in Restoration music and poetry fell within the ancients-moderns controversy. The 'doctrine' was that "words have an independent, affective meaning of their own." Concludes, "the word as the Renaissance conceived it, being an image of reason, was an inadequate vehicle for 'representing' passions."

Alexander's Feast; OR THE POWER OF MUSIQUE. AN ODE, In Honour of St. CECILIA's Day (1697):

678 Moore, John Robert. "Alexander's Feast: a Possible

Chronology of Development," PQ, XXXVII (1958), 495-8.

Cites a letter from Dryden to his sons, Sept. 3, 1697.

679   Myers, Robert Manson. Handel, Dryden & Milton; Being a Series of Observations on the Poems of Dryden and Milton, as alter'd and adapted by Various Hands, and set to Musick by Mr. Handel. To which are added, Authentick Texts of Several of Mr. Handel's Oratorio's. London: Bowes & Bowes, 1956; Folcroft, Pa.: Folcroft Press, 1970. Pp. 17-44, 83-110.

Finds that "As a musical composition . . . Alexander's Feast appears to have enjoyed only moderate success until Handel's composition in 1736 made it known to the English-speaking world."

680   Phillips, James E., and Bertrand H. Bronson. Music and Literature in England in the Seventeenth and Eighteenth Centuries. (Papers delivered . . . at the 2d Clark Library Seminar, 24 October, 1953.) Los Angeles: William Andrews Clark Memorial Library, University of California, 1954. 55pp, esp. 20-1.

Phillips's notes an echo of neo-Platonic enthusiasm in the ode.

681   Profitt, Bessie. "Political Satire in Dryden's Alexander's Feast," TSLL, XI (1970), 1307-16.

Argues that "the theme of illegitimacy and illegality which pervades the ode" satirizes William III.

682   Steadman, John M. "Timotheus in Dryden, E.K., and Gafori," TLS, Dec. 16, 1960, 819.

States that "the musical incitement to incindiarism . . . has no exact counterpart in the Timotheus legend" but comes from Dryden's reading of Boethius and Gafori's De Harmonia.

A Song for St. CECILIA's Day, 1687:

683   Fowler, Alastair, and Douglas Brooks. "The Structure of Dryden's Song for St. Cecilia's Day, 1687," EIC, XVII (1967), 434-47.

Explores number symbolism in the ode.

684 Jensen, H. James. "Comparing the Arts in the Age of Baroque," JEGP, LXIII (1973), 334-7.

Uses the first and last stanzas of the ode to illustrate the rhetorical orientation of poetry, painting, and music.

685 Levine, Jay Arnold. "Dryden's Song for St. Cecilia's Day, 1687," PQ, XLIV (1965), 35-50.

Examines Samuel Johnson's observations on the ode and analyzes its form and theme.

686 Seronsy, Cecil C. "Chapman and Dryden," N&Q, III (1956), 64.

Notes a parallel between "the refrain from George Chapman's continuation of Hero and Leander and the third stanza" of the ode.

687 Walton, Geoffrey. Metaphysical to Augustan: Studies in Tone and Sensibility in the Seventeenth Century. London: Bowes & Bowes, 1955. Pp. 83-4.

Notes that Cowley's Resurrection Ode, stanza ii, "was possibly in Dryden's mind when he composed" lines 59-63 of the 1687 ode.

On the Public Panegyrics
(See also # 851)

general studies

688 Garrison, James Dale. "Dryden and Verse Panegyric." Doctoral Dissertation: University of California at Berkeley, 1972. 448pp.

Examines the addresses to Charles II and James II in "the literary context of classical and Renaissance oratory."

689 Hoffman, Arthur W. "Dryden's Panegyrics and Lyrics," in #167 above, pp. 120-55.

Essays Dryden's virtuosity in lyrical achievement.

690 Kinsley, James. "Dryden and the Art of Praise," ES, XXXIV (1953), 57-64.

Illustrates how Dryden raised panegyric to an artful,

poetic mode. Reprinted in #177 above, 541-50.

691 Nevo, Ruth. The Dial of Virtue: a Study of Poems on Affairs of State in the Seventeenth Century. Princeton: Princeton University Press, 1963. Chapter 6.

Examines Astraea Redux, Annus Mirabilis, MacFlecknoe, and Absalom and Achitophel.

692 Parkin, Rebecca Price. "Some Rhetorical Aspects of Dryden's Biblical Allusions," ECS, II (1969), 341-69.

Discusses the "varying degrees of poetic success and the various rhetorical strategies he resorted to in fulfilling his roles as public entertaining panegyrist and apologist for Church and State."

693 Perlberg, Charley Walter. "The Public Verse Panegyrics of John Dryden." Doctoral Dissertation: Northern Illinois University, 1973. 220pp.

Examines Astraea Redux, To His Sacred Majesty, To My Lord Chancellor, Annus Mirabilis, Threnodia Augustalis, and Britannia Rediviva, to illustrate aesthetic effects and function: "to influence for the public good the behavior of the subjects praised."

694 Späth, Eberhard. Dryden als Poeta Laureatus: Literature im Dienste der Monarchie. (Erlanger Beitrage zur Sprach- und Kunstwissenschaft, Bd. 36.) Nürnberg: H. Carl, 1969. xii + 210pp.

Bibliography, 195-205. Finds the unity of Dryden's work a basis for understanding his changing opinions. Reviewed by Elmar Lehman in Anglia, XC, 403-5.

695 White, Maurice Deane. "John Dryden's Poetry of Praise: the Question of Irony." Doctoral Dissertation: The Ohio State University, 1971. 154pp.

Refutes the charges of irony and reads the poems "in the light of the classical tradition of praise and blame--the epideictic tradition."

696 Zwicker, Steven N. Dryden's Political Poetry: the Typology of King and Nation. Providence: Brown University Press, 1972. xii + 154pp.

Argues that the panegyrics can be read "as a series of attempts to forge a sacred history of the English nation." Reviewed in MLR, LXVIII, 893-4; by Eric Rothstein in JEGP, LXXII, 563-5; and, by Ted-Larry Pebworth in SCN, XXXI, #3.

on specific panegyrics

<u>ANNUS MIRABILIS The Year of WONDERS, 1666. AN HISTORICAL POEM: CONTAINING The Progress and various Successes of our Naval War with Holland, under the Conduct of His Highness Prince RUPERT, and His Grace the Duke of ALBAMARL, And Describing THE FIRE OF LONDON</u>:

697 Adams, C. W. "John Dryden's Conception of Tides," Isis, XLIV (1953), 100-1.

Conjectures that Dryden's notion of north-south tides moving from the equator to the poles may come from Roberval's explanation in Mersennes's <u>Cogita Physico Mathematica</u>, III (1647). A reply to #700 below.

698 Arber, Agnes. "Dryden and Cowley," TLS, June 7, 1957, 349.

A comment on the "star slime" image: that falling stars became jelly was a widespread belief. (See #699.)

699 Brooks, Harold F. "Dryden and Cowley," TLS, April 19, 1957,

Notes that lines 779ff. are influenced by Cowley's Davideis.

700 Dick, Hugh G. "John Dryden's Conception of Tides," Isis, XLII (1952), 266.

A Query concerning tides and the fourth stanza of <u>Annus Mirabilis</u>. (See #697 above.)

701 Kinsley, James. "The Three Glorious Victories in <u>Annus Mirabilis</u>," RES, VII (1956), 30-7.

Historical accounts of the naval battles alluded to in the poem.

702 McKeon, Michael. "Meanings of Dryden's <u>Annus Mirabilis</u>."

Examines the secondary level of the poem, "the language of eschatological prophecy which Dryden and others use in poetic speculation centering on the 'Wonderful Year' of 1666," and discusses the historical events in the poem.

703 Miner, Earl. "Dryden's Annus Mirabilis, 653-656," Exp, XXIV (1966), #75.

> Interprets the image of "the ocean leaning on the sky" as a "very fair and exciting representation of English experience of exploration."

704 _____. "In Satire's Falling City," The Satirist's Art. Edited by James Jensen and Malvin R. Zirker. Bloomington: Indiana University Press, 1972. Pp. 3-27.

> A paper delivered at the Sixth Indiana University Eighteenth Century Conference, March 16-17, 1970, discussing Annus Mirabilis and Absalom and Achitophel in the context of Pope's relationship to Dryden.

705 Novarr, David. "Swift's Relation with Dryden and Gulliver's Annus Mirabilis," ES, XLVII (1966), 341-54.

> A discussion of Dryden's poem and Swift's Travels.

706 Rosenberg, Bruce A. "Annus Mirabilis Distilled," PMLA, LXXIX (1964), 254-8.

> Examines "alchemical and astrological metaphors."

707 Scudamore, W. K. "Star Slime," TLS, June 14, 1957, 365.

> Reply to #698 above, denying a supposed Lamb borrowing from Dryden.

708 Wedgwood, C. V. Poetry and Politics under the Stuarts. (Clark Lectures, 1958.) Cambridge: Cambridge University Press, 1961. Pp. 138-73, esp. 143-5.

> Notes that Dryden's poem "is an answer, by a supporter of the Court, to the criticisms and prophecies of its enemies." Contains an examination of Absalom and Achitophel.

Astraea Redux A POEM On the Happy Restoration and Return of His Sacred Majesty Charles the Second (1660):

709 Leed, Jacob. "A Difficult Passage in Astraea Redux," ES, XLVII (1966), 127-30.

> Considers lines 159-68 "perfectly orderly."

710 Maurer, A. E. Wallace. "The Structure of Dryden's Astraea

Redux," PLL (1966), 13-20.

Finds a "Ciceronean" and "Quintillian" five part structure, which Dryden learned from his former teacher, Dr. Busby.

711 Swedenberg, H. T., Jr. "England's Joy: Astraea Redux in its Setting," SP, L (1953), 30-44.

A reading of the poem in support of the statement that "the preoccupation with the traditional establishment, a Constitutional Monarch, and with law and order," is the leit motif.

712 Wasserman, George R. "The Domestic Metaphor in Astraea Redux," ELN, III (1965), 106-11.

Notes that the metaphor "likens England's joy at the Restoration to that of a bride whose early marriage is at last to be consummated after a long annulment," and argues that it expresses "the union of God with his people."

713 Zwicker, Steven N. "The King and Christ: Figural imagery in Dryden's Restoration Panegyrics," PQ, L (1971), 582-98.

A typological approach to Astraea Redux and To His Sacred Majesty.

Heroique Stanza's, Consecrated to the Glorious Memory of his most Serene and Renowned Highnesse OLIVER Late LORD PROTECTOR of this Common-Wealth, &c. (1659): (See #s 102-3 above.)

714 Cope, Jackson I. "Science, Christ, and Cromwell in Dryden's Heroic Stanzas," MLN, LXXI (1956), 483-5.

Argues that the use of scientific figures of speech provides the poem with its structural unity.

On the Religious Poems

The Hind and the Panther, A Poem, In Three Parts (1687): (See #s 746, 756, and 761.)

715 Aden, John M. "Dryden and Swift," N&Q, II (1955), 239-40.

Suggests a borrowing from The Hind and the Panther in A Tale of a Tub.

716 Anselment, Raymond A. "Martin Marprelate: a New Source for Dryden's Fable of the Martin and the Swallows," RES, (1966), 256-67.

Discusses Dryden's fable, holding that he associated Martin Marprelate and Father Petres, the papist extremist.

717 Armistead, Jack Murray. "A Study of Structure and Poetics in Dryden's The Hind and the Panther." Doctoral Dissertation: Duke University, 1973. 299pp.

Finds that the poem's "ratiocinative pattern" is "infused with a mythic conception of reality" implicit in Dryden's religious faith "and expressed through the voice of a narrator whose personality combined the attitudes of Poet Laureate and Roman Catholic convert."

718 Budick, Sanford. "Dryden's 'Mysterious Writ' Deciphered," TLS, April 3, 1969, 371.

Argues that the Hind "fuses an invocation of an English Saint with the sacred image of a guardian angel which itself does battle with the forces of Antichrist." (Cf. the subsequent exchange of letters this TLS: Earl Miner, May 1, 466; Budick, May 22, 559; and, Miner, July 3, 730.)

719 Burnett, A. D. "An Early Verse Reply to Dryden's The Hind and the Panther," N&Q, XV (1968), 378-80.

A fable in The Lay-Mans Answer to The Lay-Mans Opinion: in a Letter to a Friend, 1687.

720 Burton, Thomas Roghaar. "The Animal Lore and Fable Tradition in John Dryden's The Hind and the Panther." Doctoral Dissertation: University of Washington, 1967. 217pp.

Holds the poem to be "a reflection of Dryden the man, his philosophy, values, and the innermost convictions of his soul."

721 Davis, Ira B. "Religious Controversy: John Dryden's The Hind and the Panther," CLAJ, IV (1961), 207-14.

Focusses on the blending of politics and religion and ties the poem to contemporary events.

722 Dillard, Nancy Frey. "The English Fabular Tradition: Chaucer, Spenser, Dryden." Doctoral Dissertation: The University of Tennessee, 1973. 220pp.

Argues that Dryden's fable is "more complicated than his predecessors'" and finds that it "satirizes the political and religious situation of 1687, while furnishing moral commentary on man's salvation in a universal sense."

723 Ellis, Harry James. "A Critical Analysis of John Dryden's The Hind and the Panther." Doctoral Dissertation: University of Pennsylvania, 1960. 307pp.

Analyzes the rhetoric, figures, and narrative frame, tone, voice and address, patterns of sound, and "the Prose Statement" of the poem.

724 Foster, Edward Eugene. "Dryden and the Poetry of Conversion: a Reading of The Hind and the Panther." Doctoral Dissertation: The University of Rochester, 1965. 244pp.

Finds a "single creative consciousness" manipulating four genres: "bestiary, beast fable, dialogue, and satire."

725 Fujimura, Thomas H. "The Personal Drama of Dryden's The Hind and the Panther," PMLA, LXXXVII (1972), 406-16.

Sees the poem as "a vivid personal confession of faith" in which "the Panther and the Hind are at times personae for Dryden."

726 Galvin, Brother Ronan. "The Hind and the Panther: a Varronian Satire." Doctoral Dissertation: Fordham University, 1961. 235pp.

Holds that "the overriding intellectual pattern in The Hind is the apology for the Catholic religion, about which all the genres and approaches, in varying degrees of relevance, coalesce."

727 Hamm, Victor M. "Dryden's The Hind and the Panther and Roman Catholic Apologetics," PMLA, LXXXIII (1968), 400-15.

Shows the influence of "English Roman Catholic apologetical writings" in the poem.

728 Harth, Phillip. "Religion and Politics in Dryden's Poetry and Plays," MP, LXX (1973), 236-42.

Reviews the third volume of #6 above, with a focus on Earl Miner's scholarship concerning The Hind and the Panther.

729 Kinsley, James. "Dryden's Bestiary," RES, IV (1953), 331-6.

Discusses the fable of the swallows.

730 Lakas, Robert Raymond. "The Hind and the Panther: Dryden's Use of the Three Styles." Doctoral Dissertation: Yale University, 1957.

731 Manley, Francis. "Ambivalent Allusions in Dryden's Fable of the Swallows," MLN, LXXI (1956), 485-7.

Focusses on lines 475-96 of part three, noting Dryden's approval of James II and disapproval of repealing the Test Act.

732 Martz, William John. "Dryden's Religious Thought: a Study of The Hind and the Panther and Its Background." Doctoral Dissertation: Yale University, 1957.

733 Means, James A. "May's Lucan and The Hind and the Panther," N&Q, XVII (1970), 416-17.

Notes an influence on line 161 of part two from Pharsalia, A_1^v (London, 1627).

734 Miller, Clarence H. "The Styles of The Hind and the Panther," JEGP, LXI (1962), 511-27.

Compares Dryden's statements in the preface with the three styles of the poem.

735 Miner, Earl. "The Significance of Plot in The Hind and the Panther," BNYPL, LXIX (1965), 446-58.

Hypothesizes that "the action of the poem is dated thus indirectly as having occurred on 6 July 1685, or more probably the night of July fifth and the morning of the sixth," the date of the 'Battle of Sedgemoor,' which, Miner suggests, is when Dryden "turned his mind toward Rome and perhaps altered at last the balance in a faith which to that time had sought the assurance of authority in religion but which previously had been weighed in favor of the religion of his national past." (See also # 138.)

736 _____. "The Wolf's Progress in The Hind and the Panther," BNYPL, LXVII (1963), 512-16.

Argues that the Wolf's "heresy" includes "political rebellion as well as the more familiar charges that Calvinistic conceptions of predestination denied the efficacy of divine Grace and the freedom of the will."

737 Myers, William. "Politics in The Hind and the Panther," EIC, XIX (1969), 19-33.

A four-part study of the political satire, noting that "Dryden's apparent frivolity in part of the poem is a calculated reaction, almost in the metaphysical manner, to the underlying seriousness of the whole work."

738 Nakano, Nancy Yoshiko. "The Authority of Narrative: Technique and Argument in Milton, Bunyan, Dryden, and John Reynolds." Doctoral Dissertation: University of California at Los Angeles, 1973. 203pp.

Finds that "By handing over the task of debate to the Hind, the narrator can maintain a stance of objectivity and disinterestedness, while nonetheless lending his support to the Hind by means of oblique commentary and strategic characterization."

739 Parkin, Rebecca Price. "Heroic and Anti-Heroic Elements in The Hind and the Panther," SEL, XII (1972), 459-66.

Argues that the first part of the poem constitutes a third genre, "neither purely heroic nor purely static."

740 Probyn, Clive T. "The Source for Swift's Fable of the Bitches," N&Q, XV (1968), 206.

Suggests a burlesque of the first 12 lines of The Hind and the Panther.

741 Russ, Jon R. ["Dryden and Topsell,"] RES, XV (1964), 303-4.

Conjectures that Hind has its source in Historie of Four-Footed Beastes, 1607.

742 Wasserman, George R. "Dryden's The Hind and the Panther, III, 1-21," Exp, XXIV (1966), #71.

Relates the passage to James II's Declaration of Indulgence.

743 _____. "A Note on Dryden's Panther," N&Q, XIII (1966), 380-2.

Cites the legend of Cadmus in Ovid's Metamorphoses, III.

as a source for lines 639-43 of part three.

Religio Laici, or A Laymans Faith (1682):

744 Benson, Donald R. "Who Bred Religio Laici?" JEGP, LXV (1966), 238-51.

Argues that the first half of the poem "was 'bred' by Dryden's reading not of Simon but of Stillingfleet and possibly Baxter."

745 Brown, David D. "Dryden's Religio Laici and the 'Judicious and Learned Friend,'" MLR, LVI (1961), 66-9.

On Dryden and Tillotson.

746 Budick, Sanford. Dryden and the Abyss of Light: a Reading of Religio Laici and The Hind and the Panther. (Yale Studies in English, 174.) New Haven and London: Yale University Press, 1970. 174pp.

Reviewed by Victor Hamm in JEGP, LXX, 670-4; in TLS, May 21, 1971, 588; and, by Richard H. Dammers in SCN, XXXI, #3.

747 _____. "Dryden's Religio Laici: a Study in Context and Meaning." Doctoral Dissertation: Yale University, 1967. 270pp.

Examines the poem's parallel with Hamon L'Estrange's Considerations, upon Dr. Bayly's Parenthetical Interlocution (London, 1651), and its indebtedness to the writings of the Cambridge Platonists.

748 _____. "New Light on Dryden's Religio Laici," N&Q, XVI (1969), 375-9.

Discusses Hamon L'Estrange (see #747 above.)

749 Chiasson, Elias J. "Dryden's Apparent Scepticism in Religio Laici," HTR, LIV (1961), 207-21.

Argues that rather than "pyrrhonistic scepticism or Catholic fideism' Dryden's adherence to the "central imperatives" of Christian humanism led to his conversion to Catholicism. Reprinted in #156 above, 84-98; and in #177 above, 245-60.

750 Corder, Jim W. "Rhetoric and Meaning in Religio Laici,"

PMLA, LXXXII (1967), 245-9.

Examines the rhetorical structure: exordium, narration, partition, confirmation, confutation, and peroration.

751 Empson, William. "Dryden's Apparent Scepticism," EIC, XX (1970), 172-81.

Examines Dryden's 'religious outlook' in the poem, arguing that his Catholic conversion was insincere. (See #s 757, 759, and 763 below.)

752 Field, P. J. C. "Dryden and Rochester, N&Q, XVII (1970), 259-60.

Sees lines 1-11 in Religio Laici as a "reply" to and "reproof" of A Satire Against Reason and Mankind, 12-24.

753 Fujimura, Thomas H. "Dryden's Religio Laici: an Anglican Poem," PMLA, LXXVI (1961), 205-17.

Argues that the opening lines of the poem reflect an accepted Anglican attitude toward "matters above reason."

754 Hamilton, K. G. The Two Harmonies: Poetry and Prose in the Seventeenth Century. Oxford: The Clarendon Press, 1963. Pp. 121-9.

Comments on the poem in the context of a discussion of rhyme.

755 Hamm, Victor M. "Dryden's Religio Laici and Roman Catholic Apologetics," PMLA, LXXX (1965), 190-8.

Enumerates "the number of Roman Catholic theological and apologetic works available to the poet in English during the years of his maturity, and the apparent echoes" in Religio Laici.

756 Harth, Phillip. Contexts of Dryden's Thought. Chicago and London: University of Chicago Press, 1968. 304pp.

Considers the religious ideas in The Hind and the Panther and Religio Laici. Reviewed by William Frost in JEGP, LXVIII, 521-4; by Margaret Lee Wiley in ELN, VI, 294-6; by Henry L. Fulton in MQR, IX, 141-3; and, by P. K. Elkin in AUMLA, XXXVI, 210-16.

757 _____. "Empson's Interpretation of Religio Laici," EIC, XX (1970), 446-50.

In a reply to #751 above, Budick disparages the notion

that Dryden espoused deist sentiments. (See also # 763 below.)

758 Hooker, Edward N. "Dryden and the Atoms of Epicurus," ELH, XXIV (1957), 177-90.

Regards Religio Laici as a "political act" and a "dramatic upsurge of intellectual forces" of the day. Reprinted in #172 above, 125-35; and in #177 above, 232-44.

759 Hume, Robert D. "Dryden's Apparent Scepticism," EIC, XX (1970), 172-81.

In a reply to #751 above, Hume argues that Dryden's conversion to Catholicism represented a sincere belief.

760 McGann, Jerome. "The Argument of Dryden's Religio Laici," Thoth, III (1962), 78-89.

761 McHenry, Robert William, Jr. "Anglican Rationalism, Right Reason, and John Dryden." Doctoral Dissertation: The University of Michigan, 1972. 230pp.

Finds a growing disbelief in the "moral certainty" of reasoning, a key factor in Dryden's religious conversion, and notes that 'reason' is "the central idea in the tone, structure, and imagery of Religio Laici, but it is a very insignificant part of The Hind and the Panther."

762 Miner, Earl. "Dryden and the Issue of Human Progress," PQ, XL (1961), 120-9.

Argues that the dim praise of reason in Religio Laici and the ironic treatment of progress in MacFlecknoe are the polarities of his faith in human progress.

763 _____. "Dryden's Apparent Scepticism," EIC, XXI (1971), 410-11.

Replies to #s 751 and 757 above.

764 Murakami, Shiko. "Kokkakyo ka Kyukyo ka--Religio Laici no baai," EigoS, CXV (1970), 10-12.

A discussion of Anglican and Catholic ideas.

765 Perkinson, Richard H. "A Note on Dryden's Religio Laici," PQ, XXVIII (1949), 517-18.

Identifies the priest as Peter Walsh.

766 Pollard, Arthur. "Five Poets on Religion. I. Dryden, Pope, and Young," CQR, CLX (1959), 352-62.

Discusses the attitudes toward enthusiasm, reason, and deism in Religio Laici.

767 Reedy, Gerard, S.J. "Noumenal and Phenomenal Evidence in England, 1622-1682," EE, II (1972), 137-48.

Notes an influence upon Religio Laici in Henry Dickinson's Histoire Critique du Vieux Testament, 1678.

768 Rippy, Frances Mayhew. "Imagery, John Dryden, and "The Poetry of Statement,'" BSUF, I (1960), 13-20.

Finds that the imagery of Religio Laici is a "perspicuous fusion of verbal precision, poetic ease, and the unerring 'eye for resemblences' which Aristotle considered the metaphorical mark of genius."

769 Welcher, Jeanne K. "The Opening of Religio Laici and Its Virgilian Associations," SEL, VIII (1968), 391-6.

Points out the similarity between Dryden's translation of the Aeneid, VI, 268-77 and lines 1-11 of Religio Laici, and notes the Dantesque use of 'Reason' as a guide to the traveler.

On Satirical Poetry

comprehensive and miscellaneous studies

770 Crino, Anna Maria. Dryden: Poeta Satirico. (Biblioteca dell' "Archivum Romanicum," I, Storia, letteratura, paleografia, 55.) Firenze: L. S. Olschki, 1958. 137pp.

Reviewed by Jackson I. Cope in MLN, LXXIV, 636-40.

771 Guite, Harold. "An 18th-Century View of Roman Satire," The Varied Pattern: Studies in the 18th-Century. (Publications of theMcMaster University Association for 18th-Century Studies, 1.) Edited by Peter Hughes and David Williams. Toronto: A. M. Hakkert, 1971. Pp. 113-20.

Contains John Dennis's letter to Matthew Prior contrasting Horace and Juvenal with a focus on Dryden.

772 Harris, Kathryn Montgomery. "John Dryden: Augustan Satirist." Doctoral Dissertation: Emory University, 1968. 232pp.

Finds that the irony of his satire "arises from the discrepancy between its artful representation, its 'wit' as Dryden called it, and that political, social or cultural reality that Dryden called 'truth.'"

773 Heath-Stubbs, John. The Verse Satire. London: Oxford University Press, 1969. Pp. 41-8.

Comments on excerpts from the major satires to illustrate Dryden's range.

774 Hughes, R. E. "John Dryden's Greatest Compromise," TSLL, II (1961), 458-63.

Notes that Dryden creates historical satire through the modes of rhetoric, "wherein he uses ridicule as a vehicle."

775 _____. "The Sense of the Ridiculous: Ridicule as a Rhetorical Device in the Poetry of Dryden and Pope." Doctoral Dissertation: The University of Wisconsin, 1954. 185pp.

776 Love, H. H. "Satire in the Dramas of the Restoration," Doctoral Dissertation: Cambridge University, Pembroke, 1964.

777 Maltby, Joseph. "The Effects of Irony on Tone and Structure in Some Poems of Dryden." Doctoral Dissertation: The University of Wisconsin, 1963. 261pp.

778 Miner, Earl. ["John Dryden,"] Symposium on Satire: Indiana University, 1970, unpublished.

Developed the idea that "satire is a deliberate act of transformation," report H. James Jensen and Malvin R. Zirker, "The Creation of the Satirist," TLS, January 5, 1973, 6.

779 Prince, F. T. "The Birth of Modern England: Dryden's Political Satires," Listener, LXIV (1960), 148-9.

780 Selden, R. "Roughness in Satire from Horace to Dryden," MLR, LXVI (1971), 264-72.

Discusses the devices of caesura and enjambment and notes that Dryden's concept of satire was nearer to tragedy than comedy.

781 Sutherland, James. English Satire. (The Clark Lectures, 1956.) Cambridge: Cambridge University Press, 1958. Pp. 49-57.

Discusses Dryden's major satires in the context of the Horatian and Juvenalian modes.

782 Wilding, Michael. "Dryden and Satire: MacFlecknoe, Absalom and Achitophel, The Medall, and Juvenal," in #167 above, pp. 191-233.

Finds that Dryden "never repeated himself" but "achieved his satiric aim in brief and never went back."

783 Wölfel, Kurt. "Epische Welt und satirische Welt: zur Technik des satirischen Erzählens," WW, X (1960), 85-98.

on specific satires

Absalom and Achitophel (1681); and, The Second Part of Absalom and Achitophel (1682): (See also #s 156, 691, 704, 708, 851)

784 Archer, Stanley. "Benaiah in Absalom and Achitophel II," ELN, III (1966), 183-5.

Identifies Colonel Edward Sackville, victor at Tangier, 1680.

785 Arnoldt, Johannes. "Das Charakterbild des Earl of Shaftesbury." Doctoral Dissertation: Universität Marburg, 1951.

786 Ball, Albert. "Charles II: Dryden's Christian Hero," MP, LIX (1961), 25-35.

History of ideas study of Dryden's development of the Christian epic hero.

787 Baumgartner, A. M. "Dryden's Caleb and Agag," RES, XIII (1962), 394-7.

Identifies Caleb as Arthur Capel, Earl of Essex, and holds that Agag was Lord Stafford.

788 Bevan, Allan. "Poetry and Politics in Restoration England," DalR, XXXIX (1959), 314-25.

Notes that Dryden was considered the preeminent satirist

of politics in his day.

789 Blondel, J. "The Englishness of Dryden's Satire in Absalom and Achitophel," Travaux du Centre d'Études Anglaises et Americaines. Aix-en-Provence: Faculté des Lettres et Sciences Humaines, 1962. Volume I.

790 Brodwin, Leonora Leet. Miltonic Allusion in Absalom and Achitophel: Its Function in the Political Satire," JEGP, LXVIII (1969), 24-44.

Refers to Dryden's "Miltonic heroics," which "have in themselves the elements of political satire."

791 Brooks, Harold F. "Dryden's Miniature Epic," JEGP, LVII (1958), 211-19.

Discusses the influence of Milton on Absalom and Achitophel.

792 Brower, Reuben A. "An Allusion to Europe: Dryden and Tradition," ELH, XIX (1952), 38-48.

Argues that "in Absalom and Achitophel Dryden affirmed an important European value: that poetic craft matters," and in support examines lines 632-59. Part of a symposium on English writers and tradition at the Modern Language Association meeting in New York, 1950, this essay is reprinted in Brower's Alexander Pope, the Poetry of Allusion (Oxford, 1959), 1-14; in Seventeenth Century English Poetry, edited by William R. Keast (New York, 1962), 375-85; and, in #172 above, 43-54.

793 Burton, K. M. P. Restoration Literature. (English Literature.) London: Hutchinson & Co., Ltd., 1958. Pp. 126-39, 223-6.

Examines the strategies of the poem, noting that it was written "in the hope of bringing Absalom to a better frame of mind, and of furthering a reconciliation between the King and the son he loved."

794 Cable, Chester H. "Absalom and Achitophel as Epic Satire," Studies in Honor of John Wilcox. Edited by A. Dayle Wallace, and Woodburn O. Ross. Detroit: Wayne State University Press, 1958. Pp. 51-60.

795 Chambers, A. B. "Absalom and Achitophel: Christ and Satan," MLN, LXXIV (1959), 592-6.

Discusses "a carefully controlled system of allusion which provides an ironic Christhood for Absalom."

796 Conlon, Michael James. "Politics and Providence: John Dryden's *Absalom and Achitophel*." Doctoral Dissertation: The University of Florida, 1969.

797 Cook, Richard I. "Dryden's *Absalom and Achitophel* and Swift's Political Tracts, 1710-1714," HLQ, XXIV, 345-8.

Finds that Swift treats Queen Anne "as gingerly" as Dryden treats Charles II.

798 Crawford, John W. "*Absalom and Achitophel* and Milton's Paradise Lost," UDR, VII (1970), 29-37.

Argues that the picture of "chaos as opposed to order" in Milton's epic suited Dryden's design.

799 Crider, J. R. "Dryden's *Absalom and Achitophel*, 169-72," Exp, XXIII (1965), #63.

Holds that the attack on Shaftesbury's son is an intensification of the attack on the father, not a "gratuitous insult."

800 _____. "Madness in Dryden's Absalom: a Conjecture," ER, XIII (1962), 41-5.

801 Cunningham, William F., Jr. "Charles Churchill and the Satiric Portrait," *Essays and Studies in Language and Literature*. (Duquesne Studies, Philological Series, 5.) Herbert H. Petit, general editor. Pittsburgh, Pa.: Duquesne University Press, 1964. Pp. 110-32, esp. 115-120.

Examines the influences of Dryden on Churchill's poetry, noting that "Dryden brought the satiric portrait to a level it had never achieved before, and his critical remarks on the subject indicate clearly that artistic motives governed his creations."

802 de Beer, E. S. "Historical Allusions in *Absalom and Achitophel*," RES, VII (1956), 410-14.

Reply to #822 below.

803 Dyson, A. E., and Julian Lovecock. "Beyond the Polemics: a Dialogue on the Opening of *Absalom and Achitophel*," CritS, V (1971), 133-45.

They discuss the relationship between history and art in lines 1-84, responding to the question, "Is the poem polemical or a triumph of form?"

804 Field, P. J. C. "Authoritative Echo in Dryden," DUJ,

XXXI (1970), 137-51.

Examines scriptural allusions in Absalom and Achitophel.

805 Fosberry, M. W. "The Case of John Dryden," OR, VIII (1968), 65-72; IX (1968), 75-81.

Explores Dryden's personal involvement with the substantive issues of Absalom and Achitophel, and compares him with Ben Jonson on the point of carricature in poetry.

806 Foxell, Nigel. Ten Poems Analyzed. Oxford: Pergamon Press, Ltd., 1966. Pp. 23-40.

807 Freedman, Morris. "Dryden's Miniature Epic," JEGP, LVII (1958), 211-19.

Discusses Absalom and Dryden's borrowings from Paradise Lost.

808 French, A. L. "Dryden, Marvell, and Political Poetry," SEL (1968), 397-413.

Compares An Horatian Ode Upon Cromwel's Return from Ireland and Absalom and Achitophel, and treats the moral framework of Dryden's political satire.

809 Graham, William. Absalom and Achitophel (John Dryden). (Notes on English Literature.) Oxford: Basil Blackwell, 1964. 99pp.

810 Greany, Helen T. "On the Opening Lines of Absalom and Achitophel," SNL, II (1964), 29-31.

Concentrates on "ironic vocabulary and mock dramatic effects."

811 Guilhamet, Leon M. "Dryden's Debasement of Scripture in Absalom and Achitophel," SEL, IX (1969), 395-413.

Argues that the "poem moves from the pretense and parody of typological interpretation to the affirmation of a rational, classical ideal in the powerful conclusion."

812 Hammond, H. "'One Immortal Song,'" RES, V (1954), 60-2.

Identifies the song in line 197 as Psalm 160.

813 Jones, Harold Whitmore, ed. Anti-Achitophel (1682): Three Verse Replies to Absalom and Achitophel by John Dryden. Absalom Senior, by Elkanah Settle; Poetical Re-

flections by Anonymous; Azaria and Hushai, by Samuel
Pordage. (Scholars' Facsimiles & Reprints.) Gainesville: Scholar's Facsimiles and Reprints, 1961. x +
11-112.

Introduction, iii-iv. A collection of some of the early
criticisms of Dryden's satire.

814 Jump, J. D. "Thomas Philipott and John Dryden. And John
Keats," N&Q, CXCVI (1951), 535-6.

Notes a borrowing in lines 156-8 of Absalom and Achitophel ("tenement of clay") from Philipott's On a Nymph,
9-11.

815 Kiehl, James M. "Dryden's Zimri and Chaucer's Pardoner:
a Comparative Study of Verse Portraiture," Thoth, VI
(1965), 3-12.

816 King, Bruce. "Absalom and Achitophel, Lines 739-40," ANQ,
VII (1968), 54.

Notes a pun on 'ayes.'

817 _____. "Absalom and Achitophel: Machiavelli and
the False Messiah," EA, XVI (1963), 251-4.

Discusses the influence of the last two books of The
Prince on Dryden's lines 230-61, and notes that Dryden
may have found another source in the case of James Nay-
ler.

818 _____. "Absalom and Dryden's Earlier Praise of Monmouth," ES, XLVI (1965), 332-3.

Discusses the dedication of Tyrannick Love and the reference to it in the satire.

819 _____. "Dryden's Absalom and Achitophel, 150-166,"
Exp, XXI (1963), #28.

Notes that the description of Shaftesbury's body shows
the Hobbesian idea of a deformity which leads to madness.

820 _____. "Wordplay in Absalom and Achitophel: an Aspect of Style," LS, II (1969), 330-8.

Lists and analyzes puns.

821 Kinneavy, Gerald B. "Judgment in Extremes: a Study of
Dryden's Absalom and Achitophel," UDR, III (1966), 15-30.

Concludes that the poem "rises above the contemporary scene and characters, biblical and epic techniques, to the statement that excess is to be condemned and the moderate position is the desirable one."

822 Kinsley, James. "Historical Allusions in Absalom and Achitophel," RES, VI (1955), 291-7.

Links Amnon, Balaam and Caleb, Agag, and Issachar to contemporary persons and events. (See # 802 above.)

823 Le Comte, Edward S. "'Amnon's Murther,'" N&Q, X (1963), 418.

Explicates line 39 of Absalom and Achitophel: Monmouth killed a watchman.

824 Levine, George R. "Dryden's 'Inarticulate Poesy': Music and the Davidic King in Absalom and Achitophel," ECS, I (1968), 291-312.

Examines "Dryden's careful manipulation of the highly allusive figura of David--particularly the Davidic code of psalmist and musician--and his symbolic use of music as an abstract harmonizing principle."

825 Lewalski, Barbara Kiefer. "'David's Troubles Remembred': an Analogue to Absalom and Achitophel," N&Q, XI (1964), 340-3.

Notes the influence of Robert Aylett (1583-1655).

826 _____. "The Scope and Function of Biblical Allusion in Absalom and Achitophel," ELN, III (1965), 29-35.

Demonstrates that Dryden's biblical allusions unify the episode of Absalom's rebellion and give it epic dimension.

827 Lord, George de F. "Absalom and Achitophel and Dryden's Political Cosmos," in #167 above, pp. 156-90.

An eight-part study of the poem in the context of "the theme of Restoration as a 'central myth.'"

828 Maurer, A. E. Wallace. "Dryden's Absalom and Achitophel, 745-746," Exp, XVII (1958), #56.

Notes that 'specious' means "resplendent winsomeness."

829 _____. "Dryden's Absalom and Achitophel, 745-746," Exp, XX (1961), #6.

Gives a seventeenth century definition of "smooth pretense / Of specious love."

830 _____. "Dryden's Balaam 'Well Hung'?" RES, X (1959), 398-401.

Identifies Sir Francis Winningham, and explicates "well hung" in line 574 of Absalom and Achitophel: "fluent or voluble and in general apt, well poised, or well put together."

831 _____. "The Immortalizing of Dryden's 'One Immortal Song,'" N&Q, V (1958), 341-3.

Identifies the song in line 197 as II Samuel xxii.

832 _____. "Who Prompted Dryden to Write Absalom and Achitophel?" PQ, XL (1961), 130-8.

Edward Seymour.

833 Miner, Earl. "Some Characteristics of Dryden's Use of Metaphor," SEL, II (1962), 309-20.

Shows Dryden to be "a creator of poetic wholes," in Absalom and Achitophel and MacFlecknoe. Reprinted in #172 above, 115-24.

834 Ogilvie, R. M. "Two Notes on Dryden's Absalom and Achitophel," N&Q, XVII (1970), 415-16.

Sees the influences of Lucan's Bellum Civile, I, 205-12, on lines 447-54, and of Virgil's Aeneid, IV, 397-8 and 401-4 on lines 270-2.

835 Peterson, R. G. "Larger Manners and Events: Sallust and Virgil in Absalom and Achitophel," PMLA, LXXXII (1967), 236-44.

Examines the work as a Roman classical poem.

836 Poyet, Albert. "Un Écho d'Absalom and Achitophel dans le Prologue d'Otway à Venice Preserved," Caliban, VI (1969), 27-28.

837 Rawson, C. J. "Beppo and Absalom and Achitophel: a Parallel," N&Q, XI (1964), 25.

Notes that the closing lines of the first stanza of Byron's poem "are a recollection" Dryden's lines 550-2.

838 Ricks, Christopher. "Dryden's Absalom," EIC, XI (1961),

273-89.

Holds that "Absalom is culpably vulnerable to Achitophel's arguments."

839 Roper, Alan. *Dryden's Poetic Kingdoms*. London: Routledge & Kegan Paul, Ltd., 1965; New York: Barnes & Noble, 1966. x + 210pp.

Reviewed by Pierre Legouis in EA, XIX, 187-8; by Arthur C. Kirsch in CE, XXVII, 644; and, by Arthur W. Hoffman in MP, LXIV, 348-5.

840 Saslow, Edward Louis. "Dryden and Achitophel: the Social Context, Historical Background, and Political Perspective of Dryden's Writings Pertinent to the Exclusion Crisis." Doctoral Dissertation: University of California at Berkeley, 1970. 370pp.

841 Schilling, Bernard N. *Dryden and the Conservative Myth: a Reading of Absalom and Achitophel*. New Haven: Yale University Press, 1961. ix + 329pp.

A critical analysis proceeding from a discussion of the intellectual background of the poem. Reviewed by Aubrey Williams in YR, LI, 618-20; by Ronald Paulson in JEGP, LXI, 643-8; by Peter Dixon in ES, LI, 69-72; and, by Samuel Holt Monk in MP, LXI, 246-52.

842 Schless, Howard H. "Dryden's *Absalom and Achitophel* and *A Dialogue between Nathan and Absalome*," PQ, XL (1961), 139-43.

Examines parallel passages between Dryden's poem and the anonymous verse dialogue of 1680.

843 Sutherland, W. O. S., Jr. *The Art of the Satirist: Essays on the Satire of Augustan England*. Austin: Humanities Research Center, University of Texas, 1965. Pp. 38-53.

Explicates the poem.

844 Thomas, W. K. "Dryden's *Absalom and Achitophel*, 581," Exp, XXVII (1969), #66.

Discusses Sir William Jones.

845 Thomas, W. K. "The Matrix of *Absalom and Achitophel*," PQ, XLIX (1970), 92-9.

Notes that the nearly 500 pamphlets published from 1679

to 1681 on the 'popish plot' were the source of the variety of Dryden's poem.

846 Wellington, James E. "Conflicting Concepts of Man in Dryden's Absalom and Achitophel," SNL, IV (1966), 2-11.

847 Wilkinson, John. "The Style of Dryden's Early Poetry and of Absalom and Achitophel." Doctoral Dissertation: State University of New York at Buffalo, 1970. 198pp.

Syntactic analysis of the poem revealing "a concealed imagery that is more akin to overt imagery in the use of modifiers, which transformational grammar shows to serve two clearly definable functions."

Mac Flecknoe, or A Satyr upon the True-Blew-Protestant Poet, T. S. (1682): (See #s 691, 762, and 833 above.)

848 Alssid, Michael W. "Shadwell's MacFlecknoe," SEL, VII (1967), 387-402.

Argues that Dryden "deliberately and ironically metamorphosed Shadwell into a humours character to show us a fool who, like the humours of his plays, persistently incriminates himself."

849 Amis, George T. "Style and Sense in Three Augustan Satires: MacFlecknoe, Book I of The Dunciad Variorum, and The Vanity of Human Wishes." Doctoral Dissertation: Yale University, 1968. 212pp.

Tabulates "patterns of stress, caesura, and endstopping; parts of speech; etymology; artificial word order; and, various aspects of rhyme."

850 Archer, Stanley. "Dryden's MacFlecknoe, 47-48," Exp, XXVI (1968), #37.

Suggests that Aston Hall is derived from Santon Hall, Shadwell's birthplace.

851 Brereton, John C. "Heroic Praise: Dryden and the State Panegyric." Doctoral Dissertation: Rutgers, The State University, 1973. 199pp.

Examines MacFlecknoe and The Medall as panegyrics, "for Dryden follows the example set by the poets who satirized Waller's Instructions to a Painter."

852 Cameron, W. J. "Dryden's MacFlecknoe: 'Keen Iambics,'" N&Q, IV (1957), 39.

Notes a source for the phrase in Cleveland's The Rebel Scot.

853 Castrop, Helmut. "Dryden and Flecknoe: a Link," RES, XXIII (1972), 455-8.

Focuses on the 1668 pamphlet, Sir William D'avenant's Voyage to the Other World, and the 1670 Epigrams.

854 Clark, John R. "Dryden's MacFlecknoe, 48," Exp, XXIX (1971), #56.

A pun on the word 'Aston.'

855 Cochran, Judith Cooley. "Dryden's MacFlecknoe and Pope's Peri Bathous as Satires on Augustan and Eighteenth-Century Literary Mediocrity." Master's Thesis: The George Washington University, 1968. 100pp.

856 Crider, J. R. The Anti-Poet in MacFlecknoe. (Brno Studies in English, 9.) Brno: J. E. Praha, Purkyne University Press, 1959. 128pp.

857 Dicks, George William. "Dryden's Use of Scripture in His Nondramatic Poetry." Doctoral Dissertation: Vanderbilt University, 1969. 256pp.

Studies the themes of "the Messiah/kingship, the Satanic, the Paradise/Judgement Day--encompassing the bulk of the poet's uses."

858 Donnelly, Jerome. "Movement and Meaning in Dryden's MacFlecknoe," TSLL, XII (1971), 569-82.

Examines the poem's structure.

859 Evans, G. Blakemore. "Dryden's MacFlecknoe and Dekker's Satiromastix," MLN, LXXVI (1961), 598-600.

Associates Satiromastix with the reference to 'prophecy' in lines 87-9 of MacFlecknoe.

860 Freedman, Morris. "A Note on Milton and Dryden as Satirists," N&Q, I (1954), 26-7.

Parallels the satirizing of Bishop Hall and Shadwell.

861 French, David P. "Dryden's MacFlecknoe, 48," Exp, XXI (1963), #39.

Speculates on the identity of Aston Hall.

862 Gamble, Giles Y. "Dryden's MacFlecknoe, 25-28 and 38-42," Exp, XXVI (1968), #45.

A note on 'supinely' and 'Blankets tost.'

863 Jack, Ian. Augustan Satire: Intention and Idiom in English Poetry, 1660-1750. Oxford: The Clarendon Press, 1952. Pp. 43-76.

Examines MacFlecknoe as a parody of the heroic style for panegyric, and essays Absalom and Achitophel as "a witty heroic," noting that "It is the prominence of the element of attack . . . that makes it a satire in the English sense of the word."

864 _____. "The True Raillery," CSE, IV (1960), 9-23.

Discusses the laughter in MacFlecknoe.

865 King, Bruce. "The Conclusion of MacFlecknoe and Cowley," ANQ, VII (1969), 86-7.

Sees the influence of Cowley's On the Death of Mr. Crashaw.

866 Koomjohn, Charlotte A. "MacFlecknoe: Dryden's Satire in Theory and Practice." Doctoral Dissertation: University of Rochester, 1971. 225pp.

Finds that the poem is a statement of Dryden's theory.

867 Korn, A. L. "MacFlecknoe and Cowley's Davideis," HLQ, XIV (1951), 99-127.

Discusses "the peculiar affiliation of Dryden's burlesque with its serious epic forerunners." Reprinted in #177 above, 170-200.

868 Legouis, Pierre. "Dryden's MacFlecknoe, 203-4," N&Q, V (1958), 180.

On "keen iambics."

869 McFadden, George. "Elkanah Settle and the Genesis of MacFlecknoe," PQ, XLIII (1964), 55-72.

Discusses the Dryden-Settle quarrel and Notes and Observations on the Empress of Morocco. (See #522 above.)

870 Miner, Earl. "Dryden's MacFlecknoe," N&Q, III (1956),

335-57.

Notes Sources in Cowley, Waller, and Settle.

871 Monk, Samuel Holt. "Shadwell, 'Flail of Sense': Mac-Flecknoe, Line 89," N&Q, VII (1960), 67-8.

Suggests a reference to Shadwell's anti-Catholicism.

872 Mullin, Joseph Eugene. "The Occasion, Form, Structure, and Design of John Dryden's MacFlecknoe: a Varronian Satire." Doctoral Dissertation: The Ohio State University, 1967. 184pp.

873 Novak, Maximillian E. "Dryden's 'Ape of the French Eloquence' and Richard Flecknoe," BNYPL, LXXII (1968), 499-506.

Discusses the attack on the poet in MacFlecknoe and in other works.

874 Schap, Keith. "A Transformational Study of John Dryden's Metrical practice." Doctoral Dissertation: Indiana University, 1972. 241pp.

How meter affects the meaning in MacFlecknoe and The Medall.

875 Smith, John H. "Dryden and Flecknoe: a Conjecture," PQ, XXXIII (1954), 338-41.

Suggests that Flecknoe's prologue to Emilia angered Dryden.

876 Tanner, J. E. "The Messianic Image in MacFlecknoe," MLN, LXXVI (1961), 220-3.

Notes that the image presents Shadwell as "an enlarging figure."

877 Taylor, Aline Mackenzie. "Dryden's 'Enchanted Isle' and Shadwell's 'Dominion,'" SP (Extra Series, Jan., 1967), 39-53.

(Festschrift: Essays in English Literature of the Classical Period Presented to Dougald MacMillan, edited by Daniel W. Patterson, and Albrecht B. Strauss.) Taylor argues that Dryden's reference to Shadwell in MacFlecknoe, 139-41, indicates that Shadwell's success with the operatic version of The Tempest "had a 'profound' effect on Dryden."

878 Towers, Tom. "The Lineage of Shadwell: an Approach to MackFlecknoe," SEL, III (1963), 323-34.

Believes that "the key to Dryden's purpose in MacFlecknoe lies in the company he forces Shadwell to keep."

879 Vroonland, James Allen. "The Dryden-Shadwell Controversy: a Preface to MacFlecknoe." Doctoral Dissertation: Kansas State University, 1972. 208pp.

Concludes that the poem "responds to Shadwell's insulting attack," summing up "years of quarrel, in that it addresses itself--albeit indirectly and by implication--to the arguments about 'plagiarism,' 'poetic license,' 'wit,' 'imitation,' 'sense,' and 'dullness.'"

880 West, Michael. "Some Neglected Continental Analogues for Dryden's MacFlecknoe," SEL, XIII (1973), 437-9.

Relates the poem to the traditions of "paradoxical encomium" and "mock-didactic," and notes that it "weaves together motifs to be found floating at large through various satiric currents of the European Renaissance."

881 Whitlock, Baird W. "Elijah and Elisha in Dryden's MacFlecknoe," MLN, LXX (1955), 19-20.

Notes that the last four lines of the poem have their source in II Kings ii, 9-15, not 12-15 as in Noyes (see #4 above).

882 Wilding, Michael. "Allusion and Innuendo in MacFlecknoe," EIC, XIX (1969), 355-70.

Discusses the allusions to "the epic and to obscenity," which Dryden used to create "the surprise and tension of wit."

883 Willson, Robert F., Jr. "The Fecal Vision in MacFlecknoe," SNL, VIII (1970), 1-4.

Argues that the "central satiric metaphor of the poem is human waste."

The Medall, a Satire Against Sedition (1682): (See also #s 851 and 874)

884 Golden, Samuel A. "A Numismatic View of Dryden's The Medall," N&Q, IX (1962), 383-4.

Describes the 'silver' medal and notes its engraving history.

885 Joost, Nicholas. "Dryden's *Medall* and the Baroque in Politics and the Arts," MA, III (1959), 148-55.

Explores the baroque rhetorical idea that "appearance transforms reality."

886 Legouis, Pierre. "Dryden's Scipio and Hannibal," TLS, July 15, 1965, 602.

Glosses lines 276-82 of *The Medall*.

887 Maurer, A. E. Wallace. "The Design of Dryden's *The Medall*," PLL, II (1966), 293-304.

Finds that Dryden used "literary conventions developed in emblematic literature and advice-to-painter poems."

888 Poyet, Albert. "A Humorous Pun in Dryden's *Epistle to the Whigs*, 1682," Caliban, VII (1970), 23-4.

Comments on the prose epistle prefixed to the text of *The Medall*: "driven to this Bay," i.e., Bayes.

889 Reverand, Cedric D. "Patterns of Imagery and Metaphor in Dryden's *The Medall*," YES, II (1972), 103-14.

Demonstrates that the patterns are "subtle and complex."

890 Roper, Alan H. "Dryden's *Medall* and the Divine Analogy," ELH, XXIX (1962), 396-417.

i.e., to "God's judgement upon the serpent in the garden of Eden."

891 Sutherland, W. O. S., Jr. "Dryden's Use of Popular Imagery in *The Medall*," UTSE, XXXV (1956), 123-34.

Discusses pamphlet literature.

892 Wasserman, Earl R. "The Meaning of 'Poland' in *The Medall*," MLN, LXXIII (1958), 165-7.

Argues that the significance to Dryden's use of the popular joke "lies in its linking the Whigs and Shaftesbury with the great remaining example of elective monarchies among the Germanic races, and not merely in its glance at the preposterous story of Shaftesbury's personal ambition to be king of another country."

VII TRANSLATIONS:

General Studies

893 Brown, Calvin S. "John Dryden as a Comparatist," CLS, X (1973), 112-24.

Discusses Dryden's knowledge of European literary traditions, his views on the relationships between literature and other arts, his comparative study of dramatic theory, and his interest in translations.

894 Feder, Lillian. "John Dryden's Interpretation and Use of Latin Poetry and Rhetoric." Doctoral Dissertation: The University of Minnesota, 1952. 199pp.

895 Fowler, John. "Dryden and Good Literary Breeding," Restoration Literature: Critical Approaches. Edited by Harold Love. London: Methuen & Co., Ltd., 1972. Pp. 225-46.

Discusses Dryden's knowledge and criticism of classical poets, noting that he "bred up their language and manners." The context is that of A Discourse Concerning the Original and Progress of Satire.

896 Ingram, William Henry. "Greek Drama and the Augustan Stage: Dennis, Theobald, and Thomson." Doctoral Dissertation: University of Pennsylvania, 1966. 191pp.

Ingram's introduction "includes a survey of the theories of translation current in the period, centering on Dryden's efforts."

897 McFadden, George. "Dryden, Boileau, and Longinian Imitation," Proceedings of the 11th Congress of the International Comparative Literature Association, Fribourg, 1964. 2 vols. Edited by Francois Joost. The Hague: Mouton, 1966. I, 751-5.

898 Steiner, Thomas R. "Precursors to Dryden: English and French Theories of Translation in the Seventeenth Century," CLS, VII (1970), 50-81.

Discusses Chapman, Pierre D'ablancourts, Denham, Cowley, and Dryden, noting that he synthesized the French theory of grandeur and the English notion of "poetic translation."

Studies of

Fables Ancient and Modern; Translated into Verse, from Homer, Ovid, Boccace and Chaucer (1700):

899 Hoban, Thomas More. "The Contexts and Structures of Dryden's Fables Ancient and Modern." Doctoral Dissertation: The University of Nebraska, 1971. 197pp.

More states, "the Fables shares enough significant features with the miscellany form as devised by Tonson, to conclude that Dryden's volume was patterned after those successful seventeenth-century anthologies."

900 Sloman, Judith. "An Interpretation of Dryden's Fables," ECS, IV (1971), 199-211.

Finds "repeated situations and character types," and argues that the work's "main action is to undermine the motives behind the violent actions of classical epic and to substitute the Christian virtues of charity and patience, which could bring about peace if they were expressed in public life."

901 _____. "The Structure of Dryden's Fables." Doctoral Dissertation: The University of Minnesota, 1968. 270pp.

Demonstrates that the "overall movement of the Fables is a transition from heroic to anti-heroic ideals" emphasized by Dryden's changes.

On Translations of Specific Authors

Boccaccio:

902 Hinnant, Charles H. "Dryden and Hogarth's Sigismunda," ES, VI (1973), 462-74.

Dryden, Furini, and the rejection of Hogarth's painting.

903 Sloman, Judith. "Dryden's Originality in Sigismonda and Guiscardo," SEL, XII (1972), 445-57.

Places Sigismonda in the line of dramatic heroines such as Cleopatra and Almeyda, suggesting a similarity between Sigismonda and Lyndaraxa.

904 Wright, Herbert G. Boccaccio in England from Chaucer to Tennyson. London: Athlone Press; Fairlawn, N. J.: Essential Books, Inc., 1957. Pp. 264-77.

Essays Dryden's handling of Boccaccio's tales.

Bouhours: (See #939)

Chaucer: (See #960)

905 Atwater, N. B. "Dryden's Translation of Chaucer." Doctoral Dissertation: Exeter University, 1969.

906 Bird, Roger Anthony. "Dryden's Medieval Translations." Doctoral Dissertation: The University of Minnesota, 1969. 219pp.

Includes The Floure and the Leafe in a study of Dryden's tales from Chaucer, arguing that "Where the medieval poems have a linear structure, Dryden provides a more unified organic line of development; where the medieval poems are populated by static figures of chiefly symbolic and moral value, Dryden creates characters that interact dramatically and whose personalities are related to the action."

907 Dobbins, Austin C. "Dryden's Character of a Good Parson: Background and Interpretation," SP, LIII (1956), 51-9.

Holds that Dryden's contemporaries accepted the version as "being validly medieval and seventeenth-century."

908 _____. "The Employment of Chaucer by Dryden and Pope." Doctoral Dissertation: The University of North Carolina at Chapel Hill, 1951. 184pp.

909 Hinnant, Charles H. "Dryden's Gallic Rooster," SP, LXV (1968), 647-56.

Identifies the rooster as Louis XIV.

910 Kinsley, James. "Dryden's Character of a Good Parson and Bishop Ken," RES, II (1952), 155-8.

Argues that the 140-line portrait fits Thomas Ken, nonjuring Bishop of Bath and Wells, and is an example of paraphrastic translation.

911 Levy, Robert Allen. "Dryden's Translation of Chaucer: a Study of the Means of Re-creating Literary Models." Doctoral Dissertation: The University of Tennessee,

1973. 289pp.

Concludes that "Dryden replaces drama-in-action with independently unified fables. His poems do not really fit his own definition of 'translation'; rather, they are newly-created poetic experiences which may stand best without reference to their originals."

912 Middleton, Anne. "The Modern Art of Fortifying: *Palamon and Arcite* as Epicurean Epic," CR, III (1969), 124-43.

Discusses the translation as a Drydenian heroic poem, noting its affective elements and the reasons it failed as an epic.

913 Miner, Earl. "Chaucer in Dryden's *Fables*," *Studies in Criticism and Aesthetics, 1660-1800*. Edited by Howard Anderson, and John S. Shea. Minneapolis: University of Minnesota Press, 1967. Pp. 58-72.

Defines the purposes guiding "numerous alterations," noting that Dryden was the "first to conceive of Chaucer as a classic."

914 Spector, Robert D. "Dryden's *Palamon and Arcite*," Exp, XI (1952), #7.

Notes that Dryden compresses four books into three and gets a better unity of action than Chaucer.

915 ‾‾‾‾‾‾. "Dryden's Translation of Chaucer: a Problem in Neo-classical Diction," N&Q, III (1956), 23-6.

Argues that Dryden's "literary conscience, aesthetic sense, and scholarly sense" dictate his choice of words.

Corneille:

916 Padgett, Laurence E. "Dryden's Edition of Corneille," MLN, LXXI (1956), 173-4.

Notes that Dryden's source for his references to Corneille was the *Trois Discours* of 1660.

Du *Fresnoy*:

917 Salerno, Luigi. "Seventeenth Century English Literature

and Painting," JWCI, XIV (1951), 234-58.

In a section on "history painting," Salerno discusses Dryden's statements in De arte graphica concerning painting and the dramatic unities.

918 Wimsatt, W. K., Jr. "Samuel Johnson and Dryden's Du Fresnoy," SP, XLVIII (1951), 26-39.

Examines Johnson's use of the preface to, and prose translation of, De arte graphica.

Homer:

919 Eade, Christopher. "Some English Iliads from Chapman to Dryden," Arion, VI (1967), 336-45.

Illustrates in four parallel passages Dryden's favorable comparison with Chapman.

920 Mason, H. A. "Introducing the Iliad (II): Pope and Dryden as Mediators," CamQ, IV (1969), 150-68, esp. 163-8.

Illustrates Dryden's command of the "middle style," noting that he "makes it possible for us to feel . . . a great moment in a great poem."

921 Smith, Constance I. "An Echo of Dryden in Pope," N&Q, XII (1965), 451.

Notes a parallel from line 117 of Dryden's Iliad, VI, in the Dunciad (A), III, 356.

Horace:

922 Maxwell, J. C. "Dryden's Paraphrase of Horace and The Staple of News," N&Q, CXCVII (1952), 389.

Sees a borrowing in line 87 of Dryden's Odes, III, xxix, and IV, iv, 61, of Jonson's play.

Juvenal:

923 Ashton, Charles Frederick. Facets of the English Way of

Life after the Style of Juvenal as Translated by John Dryden. Liverpool: by the Author, 1965. 11ff.

924 Broderson, G. L. "Seventeenth Century Translations of Juvenal," The Phoenix, VII (1953), 57-76.

925 Brooks, Harold F. "Dryden's Juvenal and the Harveys," PQ, XLVIII (1969), 12-19.

Dates the translation project back to 1687.

926 Burrows, L. R. "Juvenal in Translation," Australasian Universities Language and Literature Association: Proceedings and Papers of the 12th Congress, Held at the University of Western Australia, 5-11 Feb., 1969. Sydney: AULLA, 1970. Pp. 193-201.

927 Carnochan, W. B. "Some Suppressed Verses in Dryden's Translation of Juvenal VI," TLS, January 21, 1972, 73-4.

Using a Huntington Library manuscript, Carnochan examines "marvellous obscenities" and the mock-heroic decadence in the characterization of Messalina, excised from pp. 177, 344, 427, 435, 457, and 459 (lines 173ff., 331-6, and 424ff.) of the Dryden-Tonson text.

928 Hughes, R. E. "Dryden and Juvenal's Grandmother," N&Q, I (1954), 521.

A note on the translation of the third satire.

929 Korshin, Paul J. "Dryden's Juvenal," TLS, March 17, 1972, 307-8.

Argues that the deletions were the result of Tonson's "prudishness," not the "moral climate of the 1690's."

930 Leeson, R. A. "Dryden's Juvenal," TLS, March 24, 1972, 337.

Replies to #929 above that Dryden recognized the "obscene nature" of his verses from Juvenal VI and was self-motivated to delete them.

931 O'Sullivan, Maurice Joseph. "Dryden and Juvenal: a Study in Interpretation." Doctoral Dissertation: Case Western Reserve University, 1969. 177pp.

Finds that "Dryden had two motives for translating Juvenal's satires. The first was his belief that these poems, with their strong attacks on vice, fulfilled the proper end of satire," and the "second reason was his assertion that none of his predecessors' translations were artistic successes." Notes borrowings from Barton Holyday and Robert Stapylton.

932 Russell, Robert Eno. "Dryden's Juvenal and Persius." Doctoral Dissertation: University of California at Davis, 1966. 182pp.

Applies Dryden's prefatory remarks concerning "the poetic of satire" to the work itself.

933 Selden, R. "Juvenal and Restoration Modes of Translation," MLR, LXVIII (1973), 481-93.

Compares translations of Juvenal's tenth satire by Dryden, Shadwell, J. H., and Henry Higden, and concludes that "the scholarly classicism of Ben Jonson survived in Shadwell and J. H. simultaneous with the modern school of translators, Dryden, Rochester, and Oldham."

934 Seronsy, Cecil C. "Dryden's and Belinda's Toilet," N&Q, CXCVIII (1953), 28.

Offers a parallel between lines 133-4 of The Rape of the Lock and Dryden's Juvenal VI, 599-600.

Lucretius:

935 Austin, Norman. "Translation as Baptism: Dryden's Lucretius," Arion, VII (1968), 576-602.

Argues that Dryden's "diction and general style" resulted from his attempt to make the atheistic Lucretius acceptable "in post-Renaissance England." Austin notes 35 borrowings from Creech's translation.

936 Fleischmann, Wolfgang B. Lucretius and English Literature (1680-1740). Paris: A. G. Nizet, 1964. Pp. 223-7.

Tabulates the critical apparatus from Creech's fifth edition of De Rerum Natura, including parallels and coincidences from English poetry and contemporary English translations of the classics, such as Dryden's in the 1685 Sylvae.

937 Gallagher, Mary. "Dryden's Translation of Lucretius," HLQ, XXVIII (1964), 19-29.

Discusses how "Dryden brought to fruition in his translation certain poetic ideas which were only germinal in Lucretius."

Maimbourg: (See also #91 above)

938 Archer, Stanley. "On Dryden's History of the League (1684)," PLL, IV (1968), 103-6.

Notes changes in Maimbourg's work.

939 Cameron, L. W. "The Cold Prose Fits of John Dryden," RLC, XXX (1956), 371-9.

Discusses Histoire de la ligue and Dryden's translation of Bouhours' Vie de Saint Francois Xavier, 1688.

940 Roper, Alan. "Dryden's The History of the League and the Early Editions of Maimbourg's Histoire de la ligue," PBSA, LXVI (1972), 245-75.

Discusses Dryden's copy-text (Paris, March, 1684), and disputes the theory that Charles II had requested the translation in August, 1683.

941 Smith, John H. "Some Sources of Dryden's Toryism, 1682-1684," HLQ, XX (1957), 233-43.

Discusses the translation of Maimbourg and The Duke of Guise, I, i, noting that Dryden was reading Davila's French History, Dugdale, and whig literature.

Ovid:

942 Hopkins, D. W. "An Echo of La Fontaine in Dryden's Baucis and Philemon," N&Q, XX (1973), 178-9.

Notes the borrowing of "Full well the Fowl," etc., in Dryden's translation of Metamorphoses, VIII, from La Fontaine's 1685 Ovid.

943 Mason, H. A. "'Short Excursions' in Dryden and Pope," N&Q, XVI (1969), 341.

Notes the borrowing from Ceyx and Alcyone, 474-7, in An Essay on Criticism, 735-40.

944 Maxwell, J. C. "Pope's Statius and Dryden's Ovid," N&Q, XI (1964), 56.

> Notes that 'deduce' in Thebiad, I, 5-6, comes from Dryden's Metamorphoses, I, 5.

945 Sambrook, A. J. "A Possible Source for 'Master of the Sev'nfold Face' in Dunciad (B)," N&Q, XIV (1967), 409-10.

> Dryden's Metamorphoses, XIII, 2: "To these the master of the sevenfold shield."

Persius:

946 Frost, William. "English Persius: The Golden Age," ECS, II (1968), 77-101.

> Places Dryden in the line of English translators before and after his time.

947 Johnson, Maurice. "Dryden's Note on Depilation," N&Q, CXCVI (1951), 471-2.

> Criticizes the expurgation in Noyes (#4 above) of Dryden's footnote #7 to the fourth satire, quoting it in full.

Plutarch:

948 Pechter, Edward. "Dryden's Prose and Plutarch's Classical Mode." (Paper) Association of Canadian Teachers of English: McGill University, May, 1972.

Theocritus:

949 Gerevini, Silvano. Dryden e Teocrito. Pavia: Fusi, 1958. 29pp.

950 _____. Dryden e Teocrito: Barocco e neoclassicismo nella Restaurazione inglese. Milano: Mursia, 1966. 157pp.

Virgil: (See #s457-8 and 769)

951 Adams, Betty Smith. "Dryden's Translation of Vergil and Its Eighteenth-Century Successors." Doctoral Dissertation: Michigan State University, 1970. 221pp.

Compares eighteenth century texts of the fourth eclogue, the first georgic, and Aeneid, IV, with Dryden, noting that the "high point" of his influence "came in the mid-century in the translations of Pitt and Warton."

952 Angel, Marc D. "Five Translations of the Aeneid," CJ, LXII (1967), 295-300.

Compares translations of Aeneid, IV, 700-5, noting that Dryden "interprets rather than translates, and the net result is a new poem by Dryden."

953 Barnard, John. "Dryden, Tonson, and the Subscriptions for the 1697 Virgil," PBSA, LVII (1963), 129-51.

Discusses Dryden's profit: £ 280-320 per year.

954 Bernard, Mary L. "Dryden's Aeneid: the Theory and the Poem." Doctoral Dissertation: Cambridge University, 1970.

955 Boddy, Margaret P. "The Manuscripts and Printed Editions of the Translation of Virgil Made by Richard Maitland, Fourth Earl of Lauderdale, and the Connection with Dryden," N&Q, XII (1965), 144-50.

Discusses a possible manuscript source for Dryden's Virgil.

956 _____. "The 1692 Fourth Book of Virgil," RES, XV (1964), 364-80.

Parallel passages from Dryden's work and those "By a Person of Quality," identified as Sir Charles Sedley.

957 Brower, Reuben A. "Visual and Verbal Translation of Myth: Neptune in Virgil, Rubens, Dryden," Daedalus, CI (1972), 155-82.

Compares the theme of Aeneid, I, 124-56.

958 Cameron, William J. "John Dryden's Jacobitism," Restoration Literature: Critical Approaches. Edited by Harold Love. London: Methuen & Co., Ltd., 1972. Pp. 277-308.

Examines Dryden's political positions in the Aeneid, noting that the poem is not a "criticism of William III."

959 Fitzgerald, Robert. "Dryden's Aeneid," Arion, II (1963), 17-31.

Argues that neither Dryden "nor any other Englishman could manage except momentarily the kind of poetry required" to translate the Aeneid.

960 Frost, William. Dryden and the Art of Translation. (Yale Studies in English, 128.) New Haven: Yale University Press; London: Cumberlege; Toronto: Burns and MacEachern, 1955; Hamden, Conn.: Archon Books, 1969, 100pp.

Examines the translations of Virgil and Chaucer. Reviewed by Vinton A. Dearing in JEGP, LV, 650-1; by John C. Sherwood in CL, VIII, 255-7; by Calvin G. Thayer in BA, XXX, 91; by Reuben A. Brower in MLN, LXXI, 46-8; and, by James Kinsley in RES, VII, 316-8.

961 _____. "Dryden and the Classics: with a Look at His Aeneis," in #167 above, pp. 267-96.

Argues that "Dryden wrote his translations and many of his original poems as part of a tradition of resumed continuity in civilization stretching from Chaucer . . . to Pope."

962 Harrison, T. W. "Dryden's Aeneid," in #156 above, pp. 143-67.

Discusses the political implications in Dryden's "heightening" of Aeneas's piety, noting that he is a prince-hero "ringed by minor examples of piety."

963 Hodges, John. William Congreve: Letters and Documents. New York: Harcourt Brace World, 1964. Pp. 89-104.

Contains the Dryden-Tonson contracts for the Virgil, dated June 15, 1694, and for the Fables, dated March 20, 1699.

964 Johnson, Donald Ray. "Plowshares, Politics, and Poetry: the Georgic Tradition from Dryden to Thomson." Doctoral Dissertation: The University of Wisconsin, 1972. 240pp.

Finds that Dryden's translation of the Georgics "provided later poets with a precedent for the application of georgic themes to contemporary social and political situations, and the key principle emerging from his translation, the demand that the individual exercise control over his environment and impose his own system of order on the world."

965 King, Anne. "Translation from the Classics During the Restoration with Special Reference to Dryden's Aeneis." Doctoral Dissertation: Cornell University, 1950.

966 Løsnes, Arvid. "Dryden's Aeneis and the Delphic Virgil," The Hidden Sense and Other Essays. Edited by Kristian Schmid. (Norwegian Studies in English, 9.) Oslo: Universitets-verlaget; New York: Humanities Press, Inc., 1963. Pp. 113-57.

967 Martin, R. H. "A Note on Dryden's Aeneid," PQ, XXX (1951), 89-91.

Holds that Dryden's poem is adequate as a translation.

968 Means, J. A. "An Echo of Dryden in Pope," N&Q, XVI (1969), 187.

On Dryden's Aeneid, I, 981, and Pope's Odyssey, I, 184.

969 ---------. "Pope's 'Needless Alexandrine,'" N&Q, XIV (1967), 410.

Notes its borrowing from Dryden's Aeneid, V, 359-66.

970 Miner, Earl. "Dryden's Messianic Eclogue," RES, XI (1960), 299-302.

Argues that the fourth eclogue alludes to Princess Anne.

971 O'Connor, Mark. "John Dryden, Gavin Douglas, and Virgil," Restoration Literature: Critical Approaches. Edited by Harold Love. London: Methuen & Co., Ltd., 1972. Pp. 247-75.

Examines the relationship of Dryden's sensibility to Douglas's and Virgil's to determine "if Dryden had mistaken the nature of the work he was translating."

972 Proudfoot, L. Dryden's Aeneid and Its Seventeenth-Century Predecessors. Manchester: Manchester University Press; New York: Barnes & Noble, Inc., 1960. vii + 279pp.

A study of Dryden's sources based upon an examination

of parallel passages, centering on rhyme and phraseology. Reviewed by P. Dixon in ES, XLIX, 72-5; by Anne R. King in Criticism, III, 356-7; and, by S. Musgrove in AUMLA, XV, 84-6.

973 Sherbo, Arthur. "Virgil, Dryden, Gay, and Matters Trivial," PMLA, LXXXV (1970), 1063-71.

Examines borrowings from Dryden's Virgil in Gay's Trivia.

974 Swaminathan, S. R. "Virgil, Dryden, and Yeats," N&Q, XIX (1972), 328-40.

Notes borrowings from Dryden's fourth eclogue and other poems.

975 Watson, George. "Dryden and the Jacobites," TLS, March 16, 1973, 301.

Argues that Dryden interpreted the Aeneid as a praise of "suppressed" Augustan liberties, not of Augustus.

976 West, Michael. "Dryden's Ambivalence as a Translator of Heroic Themes," HLQ, XXXVI (1973), 347-76.

Using the Aeneid, West illustrates that Dryden's hostility toward the heroic "deepened" in his later years.

977 Wilkinson, L. P. "Virgil, Dryden, and Tennyson," TLS, Oct. 9, 1969, 1159.

Examines Dryden's Aeneid, II, 7.

978 Williams, R. D. "Changing Attitudes to Virgil: a Study in the History of Taste from Dryden to Tennyson," Virgil. (Studies in Latin Literature and Its Influence.) New York: Basic Books, Inc., 1969. Pp. 119-38, esp. 123-8.

Discusses Dryden's Aeneid in the context of Augustan admiration for Horace and Virgil, noting that Dryden "found in the Aeneid the public voice of Rome presenting in a mythological narrative the religious, political and moral behaviour appropriate to a great people."

979 Wright, John. "'Lacrimae Rerum' and the Thankless Task," CJ, LXII (1967), 365-7.

Focuses on the Aeneid, I, 461-2, noting that Dryden's version "betrays his Augustan passion for clarity."

INDEX OF AUTHORS, EDITORS, AND REVIEWERS

(By Item)

Adam, Donald G., 526
Adams, Betty S., 951
Adams, C. W., 697
Adams, Henry H., 437, 456
Adams, Percy G., 579
Aden, John M., 19, 462-5, 527, 566, 649
Adolph, Robert, 567
Albaugh, Ralph M., 123
Allen, Ned B., 369
Alssid, Michael W., 245, 342, 373, 848
Alvarez, A., rev., 3
Amis, George T., 849
Anala, Philip Z., 445
Anderberg, Gary T., 286
Angel, Marc D., 952
Anselment, Raymond A., 716
Anthony, Geraldine M., 580
Arber, Agnes, 698
Archer, Stanley, 124-5, 135, 183, 353, 528, 784, 850, 938
Armistead, Jack S., 717
Arnold, Claude, 184
Arnold, Denis, 387
Arnoldt, Johannes, 785
Arthos, John, 26
Ashton, Charles F., 923
Atkins, G. Douglas, 428
Atwater, N. B., 905
Auden, W. H., 27
Austin, Norman, 6iii, 935
Aycock, Wendell M., 423

Bache, William B., 634
Bachorik, Lawrence L., 365
Bady, Michael, 568
Baker, Van R., 389, 581
Ball, Albert, 786
Banks, Landrum, 246-7
Barbeau, Anne T., 248-9
Barnard, John, 457, 953
Barnes, T. R., 582
Bately, Janet M., 529-30

Baumgartner, A. M., 787
Beall, Chandler B., 583
Beaurline, L. A., 1-2
Benson, Donald R., 136-7, 466, 633, 744
Bernard, Mary L., 954
Bernhardt, William, 429
Bevan, Allan R., 185, 788
Biddle, Evelyn Q., 358
Biggins, D., 402
Bird, Roger A., 906
Birrell, T. A., 113, 138
Bjork, Lennart A., 467
Blackwell, Herbert R., 224
Blair, Joel, 468, 584-5
Bleuler, Werner, 250
Blondel, J., 789
Boatner, Janet W., 430
Boddy, Margaret P., 458, 955-6
Bode, Robert F., 225
Bond, Donald F., 69; rev., 19, 25
Boulton, James T., 20
Bowers, Fredson, 1-2, 94-9; rev., 5
Bowers, R. H., 469
Bowler, Elizabeth A., 251
Bradbrook, M. C., 252
Brereton, John C., 851
Brett, Richard D., 586
Brewer, Gwendolyn W., 226
Brinkley, Roberta F., 587
Broderson, G. L., 924
Brodwin, Leonora L., 790
Broich, Ulrich, 343
Brooks, Harold F., 344, 699, 791, 925
Brossman, Sidney W., 354-6
Brower, Reuben A., 28, 588, 792, 957; rev., 609, 960
Brown, Calvin S., 893
Brown, David D., 569, 745
Brown, F. Andrew, 186
Brown, Richard P., 300
Browne, Ray B., 70
Brunner, Karl, 577

Budick, Sanford, 718, 746-8
Buhtz, Georg, 143
Bullough, Geoffrey, rev., 266
Burrows, L. R., 926
Burton, K. M. P., 793
Burton, Thomas R., 720
Butt, John, 570

Cable, Chester H., 794
Calder-Marshall, Arthur, 144
Cameron, Allen B., 659
Cameron, L. W., 939
Cameron, William J., 71, 100 126, 852, 958
Campbell, Dowling, 253
Caracciolo, Peter, 101, 301
Carey, Frederick M., rev., 6i
Carey, John, rev., 153
Carnochan, W. B., 927
Casanave, Don S., 424
Castrop, Helmut, 219, 853
Cecil, C. D., 441
Chambers, A. B., 795
Chiasson, Elias J., 749
Chowdhury, Munir, 345
Clark, John R., 635, 854; rev., 6xvii, 42
Clifford, James R., rev., 19
Cochran, Judith C., 855
Cohen, Derek, rev., 18
Cole, Elmer J., Jr., 562
Colmer, John, 141
Compton, Gail H., 359
Conlon, Michael J., 796
Cook, Richard I., 797
Cooke, Arthur L., 442, 531; rev., 5
Cooke, M. G., 302
Cope, Jackson I., 145, 254, 714; rev., 146, 770
Corder, Jim W., 750
Coshow, Betty G., 360
Crawford, John W., 798
Crider, J. R., 799-800, 856
Crinò, Anna M., 102-3, 146-7, 283, 770
Crum, Margaret, 66
Cunningham, John E., 287
Cunningham, William F., Jr., 801

Dammers, Richard, rev., 746
Danchin, Pierre, 220
Davenport, Warren W., 187
Davie, Donald A., 532
Davies, Godfrey, 49; rev., 6i
Davies, H. Neville, 303-7, 673
Davis, Floyd H., Jr., 227
Davis, Harold E., 308
Davis, Ira B., 721
Davison, Dennis, 589
Dearing, Vinton A., 6, 87-8, 104; rev., 960
Dearing, Bruce, 407
De Beer, E. S., 802
Deitz, J. Eric, 228
Dick, Hugh G., 6i, 700
Dicks, George W., 857
Dillard, Nancy F., 722
Dixon, Peter, 346; rev., 841, 972
Dobbins, Austin C., 907-8
Dobrée, Bonamy, 148, 571; rev., 120, 590
Doederlein, Sue W., 470
Donnelly, Jerome, 858
Doyle, Anne T., 522-3
Dryden, John, texts, 1-41, 354, 415; reprints, 42-56; phonodiscs, 57-65
Duncan-Jones, E. E., 35
Dunkin, Paul S., 105
Dyson, A. E., 803

Eade, J. C., 519, 919
Ebbs, John D., 288
Eleanor, Mother Mary, S.H.C.J., 642
Elkin, P. K., 510-11; rev., 1, 477, 756
Elliott, Robert, 512
Ellis, Harry J., 723
Elloway, D. R., 29
Emerson, Everett H., 308
Empson, William, 751
Emslie, McD., 591-2
Enck, John J., 13
Erlich, Richard D., 188
Erskine-Hill, Howerd, 593
Evans, Betty D., 594
Evans, G. B., 106, 412, 859

Faas, K. E., 309
Falle, George G., 89, 471
Faulkner, Susan N., 149
Faulkner, Thomas C., 83
Feder, Lillian, 572, 894
Ferry, Anne D., 310
Fetrow, Fred M., 255
Field, P. J. C., 752, 804
Fiorino, Salvatore, 370
Fitzgerald, Robert, 39, 959
Fleischmann, Wolfgang B., 936
Forker, Charles R., 311
Forrest, James E., 505
Forrester, Kent A., 189
Fosberry, M. W., 805
Foss, Michael, 448
Foster, Edward E., 724
Fowler, Alastair, 683
Fowler, John, 895
Foxell, Nigel, 806
Freedman, Morris, 312, 413-4, 472, 595-6, 636, 807, 860
Freehafer, John, 374, 473; rev., 6ix
French, A. L., 808
French, David P., 861
Frost, William, 7, 313, 513-5, 946, 960-1; rev., 266, 480, 619, 756
Frye, B. J., 30
Fujimura, Thomas H., 229, 256, 725, 753
Fulkenflik, Robert, rev., 92
Fulton, Henry L., rev., 756

Gagen, Jean E., 257, 403
Gallagher, Mary T., 474, 937
Galvin, Brother Ronan, 726
Gamble, Giles R., 862
Gardner, Stanley, 31
Gardner, William B., 32, 150
Garrison, James D., 688
Gatto, Louis C., 72
Geis, Walter, 597
Geist, Edward V., Jr., 394
Gerevini, Silvano, 949-50
Germer, Rudolf, rev., 490
Gibb, Carson, 410
Goggin, L. P., 314
Gohn, Ernest S., 190

Golden, Samuel A., 357, 660-1, 884
Golladay, Gertrude L., 598
Gottesman, Lillian, 390
Grace, Joan C., 475
Grace, John W., 230
Graham, William, 809
Grant, Douglas, 8-9
Greany, Helen T., 810
Griffith, Benjamin W., Jr., 14
Griffith, Richard, 371
Grigson, Geoffrey, 33
Guffey, George R., 6, 55; rev., 6x
Guibbory, Achsah, 668
Guilhamet, Leon M., 811
Guite, Harold, 771
Guzzetti, Alfred F., 151

Haddaway, H., 266
Hagstrum, Jean H., 258, 315
Hamilton, Kenneth G., 573, 599, 754
Hamilton, Marion H., 107-8, 415
Hamm, Victor M., 727, 755; rev., 746
Hammond, H., 812
Harner, James, rev., 188
Harris, Bernard, 416
Harris, Kathryn M., 772
Harrison, T. W., 961
Hart, Jeffrey, 600
Harth, Phillip, 728, 756-7; rev., 1-2, 6ii
Hayman, John, 516
Heath-Stubbs, John, 259, 395, 643, 674, 773
Heise, Howard S., 316
Hemphill, George, 533
Hennings, Thomas P., 317
Hibbard, G. R., 666
Highet, Gilbert, 51, 601
Hill, A. A., rev., 577
Hinnant, Charles H., 366, 902, 909
Hitchman, Percy J., 391
Hoban, Thomas M., 899
Hodges, John C., 963

Hoffman, Arthur W., 152-3,
  644, 658, 689; rev., 239,
  609, 839
Höltgen, Karl J., 506
Hollander, John, 675
Hooker, Edward N., Jr., 6i,
  758
Hope, A. D., 645
Hopkins, D. W., 942
Horn, András, 154
Horsman, E. A., 155
Howarth, R. G., 459
Hughes, Derek W., 318
Hughes Leo, 191
Hughes, Richard E., 319, 650,
  774-5, 928
Hume, Robert D., 231, 404,
  476-7, 520, 560, 759
Huntley, Frank L., 534; rev.,
  477
Huneycutt, Melicent, 260

Illo, John, 449
Inani, M. M., 214
Ingram, William H., 896
Irie, Keitaro, 192
Izume, Kenji

Jack, Ian, 863-4
Jackson, Allan S., 73
Jackson, Wallace, 375
Jaquith, William G., 438
Jauslin, Christian, 535
Jefferson, D. W., 262-3
Jenkins, Ralph E., 478
Jensen, H. James, 479-80, 684
Jerome, Judson, 646
Jeune, Simon, 289
Johnson, Donald R., 964
Johnson, Ira, 308
Johnson, James W., 320, 664
Johnson, Maurice, 127, 947
Jones, Gwyn, 34
Jones, H. W., 536, 813
Jones, Richard F., 537
Joost, Nicholas, 885; rev., 7
Jump, John D., 814

Kallich, Martin, 400
Kane, Mary F., 507
Kaplan, Charles, 539
Kaufmann, R. J., 15
Kaul, R. K., 194
Kearful, F. J., 321
Keast, W. R., 74
Kermode, Frank, 602
Kernan, Alvin, 517
Kiehl, James M., 815
Killham, John, rev., 146
King, Anne R., 965, 973
King, Bruce, 156-7, 195-6,
  264, 290, 322, 361-2, 367,
  396, 417, 439, 637, 816-7,
  818-20, 865; rev., 239, 277
Kinneavy, Gerald B., 821
Kinsley, James R., 3, 21, 35,
  40, 47, 53, 75, 376, 603-4,
  690, 701, 729, 822, 910;
  rev., 6i, 19, 32, 80, 117,
  120, 146, 490, 960
Kinsley, James R., and Helen,
  36, 158
Kirsch, Arthur C., 22, 265-7,
  347, 539; rev., 6ix-x, 239,
  839
Klima, S., 323
Klingopulos, G. D., rev., 141
Knight, D. M., 6i
Knights, L. C., 605
Kolb, Gwin J., 418
Koomjohn, Charlotte A., 866
Korn, A. L., 867
Korshin, Paul J., 481, 929
Kossmann, H. A., 324; rev.,
  174, 534
Kreissman, Bernard, 114
Kronenberger, Louis, 411
Krupp, Kathleen M., 482

Lakas, Robert R., 730
Langhans, E. A., rev., 6viii-
  ix
Larson, Richard L., 197
Lavine, Anne R., 431
LeClercq, Richard V., 540-2
Le Comte, Edward S., 348, 823
Leech, Clifford, rev., 266

143

Leed, Jacob, 709
Leeman, Richard K., 543
Lees, F. N., 159
Leeson, R. A., 932
Legouis, Pierre, 419, 460,
  606, 868, 886; rev., 3, 6i,
  8-9, 80, 122, 148, 177, 534,
  599, 839
Lehmann, Elmar, 198; rev.,
  694
Lemly, John W., 363
Leschetsko, Helen, 483
Levine, George R., 824
Levine, Jay Arnold, 667, 669,
  685
Levy, Robert A., 911
Lewalski, Barbara K., 825-6
Leyburn, Ellen D., 608
Lill, James V., 199
Lindberger, Örjan, 336
Link, Frederick M., 16; rev.,
  160
Løsnes, Arvid, 965; rev., 490
Loftis, John, 6ix, 232-4,
  377-8, 544
Logan, Terence P., 461
Loofbourow, John W., 425
Loomis, E. R., rev., 141
Lonsdale, Roger, rev., 21
Lord, George de F., 827
Love Harold, 161, 235, 524,
  776
Lovecock, Julian, 803
Lowens, Irving, 284

MacCubbin, Robert P., 676
Mace, Dean T., 546, 655, 673,
  677
Mackenzie, Elizabeth, 266
MacMillan, Dougald, 6viii,
  90, 379
Mahoney, John L., 23
Maltby, Joseph, 777
Manley, Francis, 731
Marks, Emerson R., 485
Marsh, Robert H., 486
Marshall, Geoffrey, rev., 79,
  525
Martin, Leslie H., Jr., 268,
  349-50, 405; rev., 22

Martin, R. H., 967
Martz, William J., 732
Mason, H. A., 920, 945
Masson, David I., 608
Maurer, A. E. Wallace, 6xvii,
  128-9, 163-4, 432, 710, 828-
  32, 887
Maurocordato, Alexandre, 487-8
Maxwell, J. C., 401, 922, 944
McAleer, John J., 484
McCollum, John I., Jr., 291
McFadden, George, 200, 420,
  869, 897; rev., 6iii
McGann, Jerome, 760
McHenry, Robert, 162, 761
McKeon, Michael, 702
McLeod, A. L., 8
McNamara, Peter L., 236, 545
McPhee, James, 153
Meadows, A. J., 165
Means, James A., 380, 733,
  968-9
Mell, Donald C., 638
Mellers, Wilfrid, 426
Merchant, W. Moelwyn, 201
Merzbach, Margaret K., 337-8
Metzdorf, Robert F., 109
Middleton, Anne, 912
Milburn, D. Judson, 651
Miller, Clarence H., 734
Milosevitch, Vincent M., 202
Miner, Earl, 6iii, viii, 10,
  166-7, 450, 455, 547, 609-
  10, 670, 672, 703-4, 735-6,
  762-3, 778, 833, 870, 913,
  970; rev., 477
Mirizzi, Piero, 24
Molinoff, Marlene S., 269
Monk, Samuel Holt, 6i, iii,
  xvii, 77, 489, 561, 871;
  rev., 534, 841
Montgomery, Guy, 80
Moore, Charles A., 656
Moore, Frank H., 238-9, 339,
  409, 443
Moore, John Robert, 130, 203,
  364, 678
Moore, Robert E., 392; rev.,
  239
Morgan, Edwin, 237, 610
Morgan, P., rev., 477
Morton, Richard, 351

Moscovit, Leonard, 639
Mossé, F., rev., 577
Muir, Donald B., 299
Muir, Kenneth, 240
Mullin, Joseph E., 872
Mundy, P. D., 115-6, 139
Murakami, Shiko, 612, 764
Murphree, A. A., 613
Murray, Byron D., 169
Musgrove, S., rev., 972
Myers, Robert M., 679
Myers, William, 168, 737; rev., 6x, 195, 480

Nänny, Max, 490
Nakano, Nancy Y., 738
Nathanson, Leonard, 491-2
Nazareth, Peter, 325
Nelson, James E., 261
Nelson, Raymond S., 326
Nevo, Ruth, 691
Newell, Rosalie, 434
Newman, Robert S., 270, 352
Nichols, James W., 435
Nicoll, Allardyce, 67
Novak, Maximillian E., 6x, 440, 525, 873
Novarr, David, 705
Noyes, George R., 4

Obertello, Alfredo, 84
O'Connor, Marc, 971
Ogilvie, R. M., 834
Okerlund, Arlene N., 397
Olinder, Britta, 204
Oliver, H. J., 131
O'Regan, M. J., 372
Osborn, James M., 117-8; rev., 6i
Osborn, Scott C., 271
Ossenburg, F. C., 444
O'Sullivan, Maurice J., 931
Owings, M. A., rev., 320

Padgett, Laurence E., 916
Palmer, Roderick, 327

Parfitt, George, 21
Park, Hugh W., 292
Parkin, Rebecca P., 640, 692, 739
Parnell, Paul E., rev., 195
Parra, Antonio R., 170
Pati, P. K., 272
Paulson, Ronald, rev., 841
Payne, Rhoda, 205
Pebworth, Ted-Larry, rev., 589, 696
Pechter, Edward, 493, 948
Perkins, Merle L., 382
Perkinson, Richard H., 765
Perlberg, Charley W., 693
Peterson, R. G., 641, 835
Peterson, W. M., rev., 239
Phillips, James E., 680
Pinto, Vivian de Sola, 132; 3, 6i, viii, 32, 120, 122
Piper, William B., 614
Pollon, Burton R., 548
Pollard, Arthur, 766
Potter, Lois, rev., 249
Poyet, Albert, 836, 888
Prevost, A. F., 44
Price, Cecil, rev., 6viii
Price, Martin, 615
Prince, F. T., 779; rev., 616
Probyn, Clive T., 740
Proffitt, Bessie, 681
Proudfoot, L., 972
Purpus, Eugene R., 85

Ramsey, Paul, Jr., 494, 549, 617
Rasco, Kay F. D., 273
Rawson, C. J., 837; rev., 19
Read, Herbert, 574
Reaske, Christopher, 618
Reedy, Gerard, S.J., 767
Reichert, John, 398
Reinert, Otto, 328
Reverand, Cedric, 889
Rice, Julian C., 329
Ricks, Christopher, 838
Righter, Anne, 274
Ringler, Richard N., 330, 383, 652
Rippy, Frances M., 768

Rivers, Isabel, 619
Roberts, Philip, rev., 1, 6ix, 92, 117
Roberts, William, 671
Robie, B., 153
Robinson, Charles A., Jr., 41
Rodney, Caroline, 275
Romagosa, Sister Edward, O. Carm., 495
Roper, Alan H., 91, 408, 820, 830, 890, 940
Rosenberg, Bruce A., 706
Rosenmeyer, Thomas G., 6iii
Rothstein, Eric, 293, 564; rev., 249
Rudd, Niall, 518
Russ, Jon R., 741
Russell, Doris, 496
Russell, Robert E., 932

Sale, Arthur, 17
Salerno, Luigi, 917
Sambrook, A. J., 945
Sánchez Escribano, Federico, 206
Saslow, Edward L., 840
Schap, Keith, 874
Scharf, Gerhard, 207
Schilling, Bernard N., 172, 841; rev., 153
Schless, Howard H., 842
Schlueter, Anne R., 331
Schneider, Ben R., Jr., 241
Schneider, Hans, rev., 250
Schulz, Max F., 550
Schwarz, Janet Lee, 242
Scouten, Arthur, rev., 249
Selden, R., 508, 780, 933
Sellers, William H., 497
Sellin, Paul R., 498
Seronsy, Cecil C., 686, 934
Servotte, H., rev., 250
Seward, Patricia M., 340
Shafer, Yvonne B., 243
Shaheen, Abdel-Rahman Abdel-Kader, 208
Sharrock, Roger, 37
Shawcross, John T., 647
Sherbo, Arthur, 81-2, 973; rev., 153

Shergold, N. D., 384
Sherwood, John C., 499-500, 563, 565; rev., 609, 960
Sikes, H., rev., 6i
Simon, Irène, 551, 575
Simpson, Friench, Jr., 294
Sinclair, Giles M., 621
Singh, Sarup, 209, 552
Sloman, Judith, 900-1, 903
Smith, Constance I., 921
Smith, David N., 174
Smith, Denzell S., 436
Smith, Harold W., 576
Smith, John H., 6i, viii, 110, 133, 388, 875, 941
Söderlind, Johannes, 577
Sorelius, Gunnar, 451, 501
Soule, George A., Jr., 622
Späth, Eberhard, 694
Spector, Robert D., 385, 914-5
Spencer, Christopher, 427
Spencer, David G., 79
Spencer, Jeffry B., 623
Spencer, Terence, 452
Stalling, Donald L., 295
Standop, Ewald, rev., 577
Starnes, D. T., 332
Staves, Sarah S., 244
Steadman, John M., 682
Steck, James S., 111
Steiner, Thomas R., 898
St. John, L., 173
Stock, Reed C., 421
Strachey, J. St. Loe, 38
Strang, Barbara M., 553
Stratman, Carl J, C.S.V., 78-9
Stroup, Thomas B., 5, 210
Suckling, Norman, 333
Sutherland, James, 175-6, 221, 406, 446, 624, 781
Sutherland, W. O. S., Jr., 843, 891
Swaminathan, S. R., 974
Swedenberg, H. T., 6i, ii, 92-3, 177, 554, 711
Sweney, John R., 140, 178, 453, 657

Tanner, J. E., 876
Tave, Stuart, 555
Taylor, Aline M., 877
Thale, Mary, 502, 556-7
Thayer, Calvin G., rev., 6i, 960
Thomas, Donald, 11
Thomas, W. K., 844-5
Tillyard, E. M. W., 558
Tisch, J. H., 276
Towers, Tom H., 878
Tracy, Clarence, rev., 6viii
Tritt, Carleton, 211
Trowbridge, Hoyt, rev., 32
Turner, W. Arthur, 134
Tyson, Gerald, 559

Ure, Peter, 384

Van Lennep, William, 68
Verdurmen, John P., 368
Vieth, David M., 18, 222, 626, 648, 665; rev., 3
Visser, Colin W., 212; rev., 249
Von Lengefeld, Wilhelm F. K., 213
Vroonland, James A., 879

Wahba, Magdi, 214
Waith, Eugene M., 215, 277-8, 454; rev., 195, 609
Wallace, A. E., 179
Wallace, John M., 627
Wallerstein, Ruth, 653
Walton, Geoffrey, 687
Ward, Charles E., 119-20; rev., 6i, 174
Wasserman, Earl R., 662-3, 892
Wasserman, George R., 121, 712, 742-3
Watson, George, 25, 503, 509, 521, 975; rev., 3
Watt, Ian, 446
Wedgwood, C. V., 628, 708

Weinbrot, Howard D., 216, 335
Weinmann, R., 504
Welcher, Jeanne K., 769
Welle, J. A. Van Der, 180
Wellington, James E., 846
West, Michael, 217, 880, 976
Westrup, J. A., 393
Whicher, George F., 48
White, Maurice D., 695
Whitlock, Baird W., 881
Wilders, John, rev., 3, 6i
Wilding, Michael, 782, 882
Wiley, Margaret Lee, rev., 756
Wilkinson, John, 847
Williams, Aubrey, rev., 120, 841
Williams, David, 181
Williams, David W., 632
Williams, R. D., 978
Williamson, George, 422, 578, 629
Willson, Robert F., Jr., 883
Wilson, F. P., 447
Wilson, Gayle E., 654
Wilson, John H., 386, 399
Wimsatt, W. K., Jr., 918
Winterbottom, John A., 279, 296-8
Wölfel, Kurt, 783
Woods, Thomas F., 630
Wright, Herbert G., 904
Wright, John, 979
Wright, William C., 86

Young, Donald L., 182
Young, Kenneth, 112, 122
Youngren, Mary Ann, 280

Zamonski, John A., 218, 341
Zandvoort, R. W., rev., 577
Zebouni, Selma A., 281-2
Zesmer, David, 12
Zimmerman, Franklin B., 285
Zwicker, Steven N., 223, 631, 696, 713